Scaffolding

ALSO BY JANE COOPER

The Weather of Six Mornings, 1969
Maps & Windows, 1974
Threads: Rosa Luxemburg from Prison, 1979

Jane Cooper

Scaffolding

NEW AND SELECTED POEMS

Anvil Press Poetry

Published in 1984
by Anvil Press Poetry Ltd
69 King George Street London SE10 8PX

ISBN 0 85646 106 7

This book is published
with financial assistance from
The Arts Council of Great Britain

Photoset in Melior
by Bryan Williamson, Todmorden
Printed in Great Britain at
The Camelot Press Ltd, Southampton

FOREWORD

I welcome this opportunity to see my poems arranged chronologically. Both my earlier books were basically selected volumes, but they began with whatever was most recent. *Scaffolding* gives a sense of the continuous journey the work has been for me all along.

In general, poems are printed here as they first appeared. In two cases stanzas have been dropped. Where there are small changes in wording, a few are new, but most often I have gone back to original drafts of a poem and found what, to my taste now, seems a simpler or more energetic alternative. Really there is no way to revise one's younger self. Here also are eight short poems written since *Maps & Windows*, the longer poem "Threads," which appeared separately, and seven poems not published before from the years 1947-1971.

As I sorted through boxes of old drafts, I came on three attempts to write long poems about women, dating from 1953-1961. The last is the most suggestive, though broken off. "Childless, divorced, a wanderer, thirty-three" it begins, and includes the lines "The first divorce / is to be not a woman, not to make" and (speaking of the narrator's grandmother) "Once in a summer dream / she called me, *Do you love yourself enough?*" The same urgency to explore a woman's consciousness, the same need to reach a composite statement, have brought me to "Threads" and what I am working on now.

In "Nothing Has Been Used in the Manufacture of This Poetry That Could Have Been Used in the Manufacture of Bread," I spoke of how, in 1947, it was as important for me to try war poems as love poems. In 1967, anguished by United States involvement in the Viet Nam war, I opened "March" with images from other unjust wars — one recalling a nineteenth-century painting of Napoleon's retreat from Moscow, another to evoke the guilt of our long campaigns against the Native Americans. For the last few years, particularly, we have all lived with the threat of nuclear holocaust. I want just to suggest it through images of all-consuming light, rooms with only a few sticks left in them, and a stripped-down landscape that is both the joyous, essential condition of truth telling and an almost unbearable vision of the future.

Increasingly our poems question the morality, or possibility, of making poems. Yet praise has never seemed more central — praise for our earthly nature and the fragile integrity of the self. The source of love and the first care of a humane politics, they are, for each of us, momentary, to be celebrated.

JANE COOPER
New York, 1984

In memory of my parents
and for
Alice M. Boushall and Lydia Poe

The following poems have dedications: "The Builder of Houses" is for Sally Appleton. "The Earthquake" is for Kay and Byron Burford, who told me the story in stanza 1. "All These Dreams" is for Jean Valentine.

My thanks once again to my brother and the friends whose questions helped me shape "Nothing Has Been Used in the Manufacture of This Poetry...," in particular Betty Kray, Grace Paley, Adrienne Rich, Jean Valentine, and the late Muriel Rukeyser.

With regard to "Threads": My thanks to Magda Bogin for giving me Prison Letters to Sophie Liebknecht; to May Stevens, who first showed me the faces of Rosa Luxemburg and whose collage "Two Women" proved an essential text; and to Grace Paley and Jean Valentine for phrases that seemed to illuminate Rosa Luxemburg's ecological concern and became deeply part of the poem.

J.C.

CONTENTS

1
Mercator's World

1947-1951

For a Boy Born in Wartime

Head first, face down, into Mercator's world
Like an ungainly rocket the child comes,
Driving dead-reckoned outward through a channel
Where nine months back breath was determined
By love, leaving his watery pen
—That concrete womb with its round concrete walls
Which he could make a globe of all his own—
For flatter, dryer enemies, for home.

Boy we have set in motion like an engine,
Bound by our instruments no one knows where
Until upending you are zero London,
Headlong from water, what will you make of air?
An empire? light to whistle through? a ball
To bounce? Or will your tumbling feet
Drop down and inward to the concrete
Unmalleable mirror world we live in,

Inheritor of our geographies,
Just as we rise to slap your fluttering cry?

Eve

Now she is still not beautiful but more
Moving than before, for time has come
When she shall be delivered; some-
one must have, move her, or the doors
Be shuttered over, the doorlids shut, her
Eyes' lies shattered. In the spume
Of a triple wave she lives: sperm,
Man and life's mate break like flags upon her shore.

Marriage must take her now, or the sly
Inquirer, inviting her to ship for his sake,
Will share all islands inland with her, her sky
No one else shares, will slake
Conquerlust. Seas wash away her ties
While through her thigh-trees water strikes like a snake.

The Door

Intelligent companion,
Talented—yes, and blind—but can
I live the pitiful part I play?
For what do you see when I
Come to you? Isn't it woman,
Passion, a pair of eyes, the ground
To prove old sex and sorrows on?
Tomorrow, if you were blinded
Really, physically, could you
Picture me as I come through
This door? Could you construct a me,
All physical reality,
And then, easy as light,
Penetrate the lips I speak from,
Plant them with speech or start
Thought with your kisses?
                              I am
A person after all. You are
A person. We are proud and fear
The same things: pride of possession,
Cowardice, communication
Stopped.
             Silhouetted in this door
I stop a moment like a stranger
Before the darkness. What do you see?
I wait for eyes, then tongues to join,
Intelligent, companions.

Song

Here I am yours, and here, and here:
In body, wit and in responsibility.
And here I am not yours: inquire
Of my first lover for my fire
And of my second for my subtlety.

In the menagerie of thought
You own the elephant but not the man,
But since humanity grew out
Of the same cell, of the same root,
Why do you cry? You suck the larger crumb,

Move through the larger rooms, explore
The earliest if not the dark, dark continents;
And what you have I had before
Either my subtlety or fire:
Brutal before Biblical innocence.

Twins

You ask for love but what you want is healing,
Selfishly, understandably. You pray
For marriage as another man might pray
For sleep after surgery, failing
More ether, miraculous cure by a saint
Or the tissues still uncut. You want
Never again to look at incompleteness,
Yours or mine or ours; this is our weakness.

All the images you use are of darkness—
Sleep, forgiveness, physical unity
Transcending daylight bodies and the rays
Where a Curie works or wounded priests confess.
You won't believe you're maimed, you won't believe
There is any other way to live
Than whole. You're as careful of your honor
As any cripple; this is our humor.

But I'm ashamed—shamed by the doctors
You've prayed to in the hope someone might close
Your eyes in passion, shamed that I expose
And kill and heal you with the simplest finger.
I'm radium, apocalypse in the breast;
I understand—this is my selfishness.
And while love dies cancered by light, I
Hesitate and can neither live nor die.

The Knowledge That Comes Through Experience

I feel my face being bitten by the tides
Of knowledge as sea-tides bite at a beach;
Love leaves its implications, wars encroach
On the flat white square between my ear and jaw
Picking it as the sea hollows out sand....
I might as well stick my head in the maw

Of the ocean as live this generously:
Feelings aside I never know my face;
I comb my hair and what I see is timeless,
Not a face at all but (besides the hair)
Lips and a pair of eyes, two hands, a body
Pale as a fish imprisoned in the mirror.

When shall I rest, when shall I find myself
The way I'll be, iced in a shop window?
Maybe I'll wake tonight in the undertow
Of sleep and lie adrift, gutted helpless
By the salt at my blue eyes—then the gulfs
Of looks and desire will shine clean at last.

Meanwhile I use myself. I am useful
Rather foolishly, like a fish who yearns
Dimly toward daylight. There is much to learn
And curiosity empties our rewards.
It seems to me I may be capable,
Once I'm a skeleton, of love and wars.

Long View from the Suburbs

Yes, I'm the lady he wrote the sonnets to.
I can tell you how it was
And where the books lie, biographies and his
Famous later versions now collected
In one volume for lovers. (You
Can never really analyze his method

If you only read those.) Once for instance
He begged to meet me under an oak
Outside the city after five o'clock.
It was early April. I waited there
Until in the distance
A streetlight yielded to the sensual air.

Then I walked home again. The next day
He was touchy and elated
Because of a new poem which he said
Marked some advance—perhaps that "honest" style
Which prostitutes our memories.
He gave it to me. I said nothing at all

Being weary. It had happened so often.
He was always deluding himself
Complaining (honestly) that I spurned his gifts.
Shall I tell you what gifts are? Although I said
Nothing at the time
I still remember evenings when I learned

The tricks of style. Do you know, young man,
Do they teach you in biographies
How it feels to open like a city
At the caress of darkness, then sickening
To walk about alone
Until a streetlamp yawns in reckoning?

After the Bomb Tests

1

The atom bellies like a cauliflower,
Expands, expands, shoots up again, expands
Into ecclesiastical curves and towers
We pray to with our cupped and empty hands.
This is the old Hebraic-featured fear
We nursed before humility began,
Our crown-on-crown or phallic parody
Begat by man on the original sea.

The sea's delivered. Galvanized and smooth
She kills a tired ship left in her lap
—Transfiguration—with a half-breath
Settling like an animal in sleep.
So godhead takes the difficult form of love.
Where is the little myth we used to have?

2

Where is the simple myth we used to have?
The childish mother and her fatherless son,
That infinitesimal act, creation,
Which shocks two cells so that they melt and solve
A riddle of light and all our darkness tears
With meanings like struck water round a stone?
Is it all gone? Are the meanings gone?

I walk out of the house into the still air,
Moving from circle to circle—hot, cold,
Like zones of water this October night.
All the stars are still arranged in spheres,
The planets stalk serenely. Thinking of Kepler
I pick a grassblade, chew it up, then spit.
Now I have thought, he said, *the thoughts of God.*

3

Now I have thought the very thoughts of God!
Mentally checking the sky he doused his lamp
And let the worlds come to life inside him.
And if he were wrong? Could one harmony hold
The sum of private freedoms like a cup?
He glanced outward. Affectionately, delicately,
Distance received him in a lap of sleep;
He felt its warm muzzle on his eye.
He smiled, darkening. He had caged the sky.

When he woke up dawn stretched like a canvas,
Empty and deep. Over the slick seal river
A wind skated. Kepler, curious, rose,
Started to cross himself—then like a lover
Or virgin artist gave himself to his power.

In a Room with Picassos

Draw as you will there are no images
Which exactly reproduce this state of mind!
No bull can satisfy my unspoken anger
Or Spanish boys speak plainly for my love
While you refuse it. I can stand and stand
In front of canvas and artistic paraphernalia
But nothing there will answer me with pride:
I am the exact shade of shame and desire,
Your justification in the face of his
Simple indifference to simple fire.
I am the offering which always moves
Anyone, no matter how far away he is from love.

Gaza

Too calm to beg for pity yet too strained
Ever to call my bluff or disown me
Openly, you said nothing but remained
Masterful—I thought weak—solitary,
Like one of those old kings without a face
Who flank in tiers of weatherbeaten stone
The O of a cathedral carapace:
Unmouthed, you groped like Samson to be dethroned.

Meteors

Whom can we love in all these little wars?
The aviator, king of his maps and glowing lights
But dispossessed of six-foot-two of ground?
The sailor, blind as a worm, suspended
In a hammock made of scrap iron, in his fear
Heavy and liquid to the touch as night?

Whom can we love? The same question
Asked five years back drops through my ear and dies
With a fizzle of brightness at the center of my brain.
The sky is streaked with pilots falling. I see
Buried in altitude like meteors
Cartoons of wit and sex, skeletons of leaders.

Obligations

Here where we are, wrapped in the afternoon
As in a chrysalis of silken light,
Our bodies kindly holding one another
Against the press of vision from outside,
Here where we clasp in a stubble field
Is all the safety either of us hopes for,
Stubbornly constructing walls of night
Out of the ordered energies of the sun.

With the same gratitude I feel the hot
Dazzle on my eyelids and your hand
Carefully opening my shaded breasts.
The air is very high and still. The buzz
And tickle of an insect glow and fuse
Into the flicker of a pulse. We rest
Closed in the golden shallows of a sound.
Once, opening my eyes, I receive your trust.

My fingers pick at a broken shining blade
Of stubble as you bend to look at me.
What can I do to help you? Some extreme
Unction of the act of love is on us.
The act itself has built this sphere of anguish
Which we must now inhabit like our dreams,
The dark home of our polarities
And our defense, which we cannot evade.

2
Nothing Has Been Used in the Manufacture of This Poetry That Could Have Been Used in the Manufacture of Bread

1974

A LONG TIME AGO I had a student who was married to a tugboat captain. She had three babies and used to get up at five in the morning to work on her stories before the children woke. The reasons why she was finding it hard to do the writing that was in her were not far to seek, yet she and her husband looked forward to a still larger family. I have no idea what happened to that young woman; perhaps she is back at the typewriter now, with the last child in school. But more than two decades of teaching women—talented, intellectually curious and passionately eager to live their lives—have convinced me she's not an isolated example. Tillie Olsen, in particular, has written movingly of the "Silences When Writers Don't Write," of women's silences, and at the same time of her own desire to cry out at H.H. Richardson (who said, "There are enough women to do the childbearing and childrearing. I know of none who can write my books."): "Yes, and I know of none who can bear and rear my children either!"

Women, surely, have always written—just as in preliterate times they must have been storytellers and weavers of legends alongside men. But if this is true, why did so many stop? Or, if they kept on, why didn't more of them publish? Such questions are very much in the air right now, and the commonest answer, following Olsen, is that marriage along the old, accepted lines and, especially, childbearing and childrearing can sap energy, privacy, a sense of the earned right to write. The last invasion may well be the most serious one. "Them lady poets must not marry, pal," says John Berryman's Henry, suggesting also—but don't we all recognize, even today, the unfitnesses he suggests?

I've never married, have no children, so you could say my case was always different. Yet from the age of twenty-two to the age of twenty-six, I worked strenuously and perfectly seriously on a book of poems (a *book*, not just poems), then "gave up poetry" and never tried to publish but one of them. Why? Does this mean the same injunctions have affected all women, not just the wives and mothers? Haven't we been most deeply shaped in our very expectations of ourselves, and isn't this what has been most daunting? In fact, since I was unmarried and belonged to a marrying generation, was I in a special way vulnerable to the unspoken words: "What sort of woman are you?"

While I was working on my book, I told people I didn't believe in magazine publication because all my poems were related. Privately, I felt the poems were never finished. I suspect most privately of all, I couldn't face living out the full range of intuition they revealed. Later, after I'd come back to writing and was beginning to publish in magazines and an occasional anthology, the old poems still seemed to throw off balance whatever I was currently doing. After 1956 or so, I only remember looking at them once until recently. For a while I believed I'd destroyed them. They turned up on a lower shelf of my bookcase, in an old Christmas card box, along with drafts and drafts of later and often less striking work.

In the winter of 1971-72, friends looking at some new manuscripts of mine told me I was changing. The new poems seemed more tense, more aggressive than those in my first collection, *The Weather of Six Mornings*, written mostly during my thirties and finally published in 1969. And it's true that book is full of acceptances, even pieties, and not just formal ones. Above all the self is seen as no more important than anybody else, a self in a world of selves who give one another strength and life. (One poem, for my mother, ends "Which one of us is absent?" The book ends "why should I sign / my name?") I said no, I thought I was just getting back to something closer to the mood of my earliest work. Earliest work? I hesitated, made excuses, but before long the living-room floor was carpeted with dozens of old yellow scratch sheets.

Now I was the one to be surprised. For one thing, there were many more poems than I'd imagined: eighty-odd in all. Then, there were some good, complete poems I had no recollection of writing. It was a shock to discover that at some point, probably in the mid-fifties, I'd thought enough of the poems to go through and date a number of them; also that where various drafts existed, I'd as often as not made a poem less rather than more interesting. Some poems got angrier and sharper and less abstract as they went along, but others lost their initial honesty and became over-complicated. This was particularly true of poems which I'd tried to rewrite between 1952 and 1954, after the impulse toward that first collection was spent. Finally, it was a shock to find that I'd forgotten, or distorted, or perhaps never truly faced what the book was "about."

What I Had Told Myself

What I had told myself, what I remember telling myself in my twenties, was that I was writing a book of war poems from a civilian's, a woman's, point of view. World War II was the war I grew up into. I was fourteen when England and France declared war on Germany (and I came from a fiercely internationally minded, interventionist family, except that my brother, just older than myself, was for a short time a pacifist); I was seventeen at the time of Pearl Harbor; the first atomic bombs were dropped on Hiroshima ͟ͅnd Nagasaki, and peace treaties were signed, just before my senior year in college. From 1946 to 1950, those intense writing years, I lived in Princeton, which was full of returned veterans studying on the G.I. Bill. I was even an associate member of a veterans' group which met to discuss issues like the implementation of the Marshall Plan. In the summer of 1947 I went to England and France before it was possible for an American to do so without a reason recognized by the host government. I went to study at the first Oxford summer school, along with many students and professors from the great pre-war universities of Europe. These men and women, in their heavy sandals and worn, stained shirt collars, I found in a state of euphoria because they could talk to one another for the first time in eight years. London was still full of bombed-out sites being converted into car parks, except that there were few cars. Wherever I walked a single hammer could be heard tapping. In late August I crossed the Channel. At Boulogne the only solid things left in the landscape were the German fortifications and submarine pens, with here and there a foundered Allied invasion ship. Elsewhere along the French coast the V-2 rocket pens still humped up like molehills made of cement. In Paris I saw a sign in a department-store window that read, over a display of wicker furniture: NOTHING HAS BEEN USED IN THE MANUFACTURE OF THIS FURNITURE THAT COULD HAVE BEEN USED IN THE MANUFACTURE OF BREAD.

How everything looked, what the European professors said, changed my life, quite simply. I find I wrote home in the middle of that summer: "I woke the other morning with the realization that I should have to write, and probably write poetry. This made me feel foolish, more than anything else. I distrust poets, and have been fighting the idea for about five years now. Just as I have been fighting the idea of teaching. But perhaps they are both necessary."

At Oxford our tutors were members of the Oxford Extra-Mural Delegacy, which during the winters sent men and women into rural villages to conduct workers' education courses in literature, history, social philosophy, that were to run for four consecutive years. This project had the blessing of the post-Churchill Labour Government. It was a kind of teaching I had never really imagined, despite having graduated from a midwestern state university which had a whole campus dedicated to agronomy, for the sake of its constituent farmers, and ran "short courses" in cheese-making. At Oxford also our tutors read poetry aloud to us in the evenings, something that rarely happened in those days in the United States; readings, like chamber music, had been popular in the bomb shelters, the Underground stations, during the London blitz. The European professors never tired of quoting poems to one another in Czech, Russian or Polish, French. For the first time poetry presented itself to me as a means of survival.

So I came home in September not to start to write (for I had written poems all during high school and had recently begun again after a long wartime silence) but with a focus.

This war had been, I thought, peculiarly a civilians' war, the war of the bombed-out cities and of ruined, isolated country houses in northern France. Even now, two years later, the dark bread, made of potatoes or sometimes even sawdust, flattened almost to the tabletop when you pressed it with a sharp knife.... I thought, at the same time, that all wars are probably total for the people living through them; the Hundred Years' War must have been a total civilians' war. For civilians, read women—women-and-children, women-and-the-sick-and-the-old. Yet of course, women had not just been civilians during World War II, not just the passive receivers of suffering. At Oxford I knew a young Frenchwoman who had been a member of the Resistance; my best English friend was just out of the WRENS, the women's branch of the Royal Navy. I had myself spent several terms at college studying to be a meteorologist— astronomy, navigation, physics—with the difference that I hadn't really needed to, in America where women were never drafted, and after a while I had switched to languages, with some vague idea (since I imagined the war would go on and on) of a translating job in Washington.

I would write as a noncombatant, a witness. It was the air war I was most haunted by, since my brother, my father, my uncle, my brother-in-law had all been involved in aviation in some form during the war years. I never could get over the peculiar beauty of a bombed-out landscape (which needless to say I only saw once the worst had been cleaned up, once the summer field flowers—poppies and fireweed and ragwort—had seeded themselves and started blooming over the rubble); nor my guilt because I found the desolation visually beautiful. I had two friends from childhood, now returned veterans, who had been shot down as pilots over Europe and imprisoned; one later made his way to Ravensbruck and helped repatriate French survivors of the concentration camp there. I hated the very idea of war, all its details, yet obviously, I was excited and absorbed by it, and also I felt guilty because I had not participated in any direct way, only through association. And how could you write except from experience?

Perhaps, as Grace Paley has suggested, this was one of the true problems of women writers at that time. The men's lives seemed more central than ours, almost more truthful. They had been shot down, or squirmed up the beaches. We had waited for their letters. Again, I was not a European or an Englishwoman. Yet when I hesitated to comment on Dylan Thomas's "A Refusal to Mourn the Death, by Fire, of a Child in London," then quite a new poem, in my Oxford seminar, because I had not lived through the blitz, my tutor said soberly,"Thank God you were spared that."

And even now I have to ask myself: Why did I feel the need to write about the holocaust almost more than individual human relations, or, to disguise my purpose to myself? What fascination with the will, as well as sympathy, did that reflect?

Hearing poems read aloud in the long, light Oxford evenings brought not only Thomas but, even more vividly, Hopkins and Yeats alive for me. Was it for this reason, I wonder, that all the poets I turned to when I started to write again were neither Americans nor women? What would have happened if I'd listened to William Carlos Williams instead, with his love for casual American speech rhythms, or if I'd valued Emily Dickinson more? Auden was out of favor in England when I was there, because after serving as a model of political engagement during the thirties, he had come to the United States just before the outbreak of World War II, thus escaping much of what he had helped others prepare their minds for. A cop-out, it seemed to the young tutors, who stubbornly read us Day Lewis and MacNeice instead. But I'd long been familiar with the work of Auden and also Spender, and when I thought of a contemporary, politically aware tone of voice, that was the tone I still thought in. Because of my work in languages, I was also steeped in the poetry of García Lorca, with its mixture of surrealism and peoples' theater, but it was only much later that I could begin to understand what that combination might mean to me.

"A Book of War Poems"

Had I published my book of poems in 1950 or '51 or '52, as I
suppose could have happened, it would certainly not have
been the same collection I now call *Mercator's World*. It
would have been longer, rougher and more mixed in tone,
and it would have contained many more political poems. It
would have been more like (though still not clearly) "a
book of war poems from a woman's point of view." For
especially to begin with, war and its survivors made up
much of my conscious subject matter; and even my imagery
(which is not, as Adrienne Rich has pointed out, a product
of our conscious choice so much as it is something thrown
up on our consciousness, like our dreams) was dominated
by explosions, mapmaking and stars and navigation, and
scientific discovery. I was writing with a curious amalgam
of seventeenth-century and twentieth-century references.
Behind the American atomic-bomb tests in the Pacific in
1946, I perceived the *hubris* of Kepler (nevertheless a
genuinely religious man), and the fact that the first silk I
saw after five years of wartime was a parachutist's landing
chart, made into a woman's headscarf, somehow got mixed
up in my mind with my father's collection of early European
maps of the discovery and colonization of Florida. Most of
these maps were based on Mercator's projection, with its
squared-off yet strangely exaggerated perspectives. If
"Mercator's world" was in an obvious sense my father's
world, it also suggested a habit of thinking which, distorted
and then followed down to its logical end (as Einstein's
theory prepared the way for the hydrogen bomb, which
Einstein denounced), had plunged us into global conflict
for the second time in a generation.

Not that my imagery was only a kind of large abstract
grid taken from warmaking and the physics of fission and
light. There are also specific human images in many of the
early poems that still have the power to take me a bit by
surprise and so to move me.

> In bomb shelters many are honest
> As Jews are
> Pierced by the knowledge of bullets in bullet-proof cars.

was written even before I went abroad. Until I came on a line about German children holding out their palms to beg as a closed train blurs by, I'd forgotten that civilian trains were still sealed in the Occupied Zones in 1947. And an ex-P.O.W. reentering New York

> ...like a man off an operating table
> A tangible silence around him, an ether cone,
> While American tastes and words in his mouth glitter
> Like knocked-out teeth...

is dazed by his own inarticulateness: "his bell of glass / Which keeps even the girls he kisses from touching his face."

Perhaps it is important that these poems were begun in a climate which, while it countenanced—with a good deal of protest—the Bikini bomb tests, also saw the making of the United Nations, the Marshall Plan and other schemes for the reconstruction of Europe, and not long afterward the first Fulbright scholarships. And although the reasons were certainly more personal than political, I wonder if it is wholly irrelevant that the poems ended, trickled away, at about the point when the McCarthy hearings became possible?

Now that we turn against the whole notion that the United States should be a moral leader in world affairs—as if we could tell others what to feel and how to govern themselves—it's hard to remember the optimism and seriousness of the first couple of years after the end of World War II, when many people, including many returned veterans, felt responsible for rebuilding Europe and Japan physically and economically and, above all, for restoring communications among nations. I think some of that optimism got into my poems, at least in the form of a confidence that I could write them. Several are positive statements of international responsibility. At the same time, there is some hopelessness that we (that is, Americans), or at least I myself, could ever rise above the fact that our experiences had *not* been those of the damaged civilian populations:

> For past a certain knowledge
> Of headlines there can be no sharing....
>
> And Europe's children cease to live
> For a moment in our minds
> And a certain bombed corner kind-
> ly obliterates itself....

It was a celebration of spring, that poem!

Another poem asks what happens to peasants in a war ("Women go / On sweeping out the house where they were killed"), while exploring the state of mind of the wisest human beings, which I saw as a kind of recovered innocence, knowledge tempered by extremes of mental and physical suffering. I couldn't forget the two Czech professors in my Oxford seminar who, even in 1947, no longer looked forward to political freedom but used to argue endlessly over how, under totalitarian conditions, one could preserve freedom of the spirit. I concluded that "Universal concern is not enough." "The great gas chambers of the mind shut down" on whatever we fail to accomplish in our own persons. Struggling to define my own religious consciousness between the poles of Christianity and Existentialism, I prayed, "Why, while cities burn, do I still live?"

> I have no faith. I do not expect to recover
> Any but myself, the unit, man.
> Mass charity affects me like an ether
> Empty of consciousness as of its pain.

The Archipelago of Love

"Not enough scherzi," said my brother affectionately, when my 1969 book came out, and indeed I consider it a great weakness in my writing that I'm so shy about dealing with joy. For I've known real joys in my life, and the period I'm

27

talking about was unusually full of them. The war, though it obsessed me, was over. Horizons were expanding not only geographically and politically but personally for me. The men were back. I was living in a men's university town. When I think of the year 1948, I can hardly remember times when I was alone (though there must have been some, while I worked on my poems or finished another half-day's stint of freelance editing). What I remember instead is tramping across fields or driving in an open car with one companion or another; climbing the scaffolding of some new postwar housing because I was excited about architecture; sitting in on seminars on literature or philosophy and then talking afterward under a dogwood tree or hunched over bowls of homemade soup at a student restaurant. Or, later, when it seemed as if some kind of decision must be drawing near, there were the evenings of mutual silence and intense, diffident questionings.

Marriage was on everybody's mind in those days, men's as well as women's, after the fragmentation of the war, and most of my friends wanted three or four babies as soon as they could afford them. For the veterans studying on the G.I. Bill, there was a rush to put down roots, to "get started." Still, it was curiously difficult, if you hadn't married during the war, to imagine how a peacetime relationship could develop slowly and quietly and reach fruition without the drastic backdrop of wartime leaves, wartime ultimatums. I sometimes wonder if I knew how to make a decision for several years after I stopped reading casualty lists. On the windowsills of the dormitories were large metal stars giving the names of former Princeton students who had occupied rooms there and been killed; often they were names I knew. Yet I used to feel a kind of outrageous triumph, an elation that seemed as if it would grow and grow and might take over everything. I was young, alive, free, learning to know myself and others, learning my craft of poetry, all my senses were opening.

So, no matter what headlines I gave my work, from the first I was exploring other territory: "Look where the archipelago of love / Lies at our feet, the waves washing like fever, / Conscious, unconscious...." The earliest complete poem in this volume, "Eve," written when I was just twenty-three, is a poem of sexual awakening, frankly acknowledged. "In the spume / Of a triple wave she lives: sperm, / Man and life's mate break like flags upon her shore." What can I say now to those images of conquest? At the same time the sexual over-view ("Marriage must take her now, or...") shows how much I was still living within a social pattern, or at least a pattern of expectation, as clearly defined as the physical world had once seemed to be according to Mercator's projection. Out of the tension between that enclosing, conservative order and my own expanding vision and senses came what I later recognized to be the strongest pages of my abandoned "book."

For here, as was not true of the war poems, there could be no question of authenticity. Despite the limitations on sexual roles which the poems alternately question and confirm, relationships between women and men are seen in individual terms and, increasingly, with unsparing eyes. It was in 1948 that I wrote "The Door" (other versions speak of "this double door"), which is a plea for equality and for not being treated as a sexual object. While this poem seems simply honest today, I wonder how it would have sounded had it been published at the time? Interestingly, I wasn't really able to deal with all it said myself. The draft I finally settled on cut out the lines "I am / A person after all, you are / A person..." and substituted at the end a vision of almost supernatural union. Having asked the man not to be a god, did I get scared? Somehow I was trying, in imagination, to revive some perfect model of the trap I needed to spring.

Perhaps not surprisingly, poems that promised most in the way of love and growth were often distanced by their forms. This too was part of the world, social and literary, that surrounded me. Probably it was also part of my own mind-set. "Eve" is modeled on sonnets by Hopkins. I wrote a lot of songs, following seventeenth-century examples as well as Yeats and Auden. These stay with me now mainly for what they reveal in spite of, not because of, their manners.

"I guard my independence / Which beautifully guards / Me..." seems chilling in its implications. More sympathetic is a song written for a friend on his thirtieth birthday, though again, I can't help speculating on what it might have meant to other women had it come out when it was composed:

> En l'an trentiesme de mon aage
> Perhaps I shall be wiser,
> More certain than I am here
> In the coils of my heritage.
>
> Que toutes mes hontes j'eus bues—
> At twenty-three
> I am caught in such necessity
> To be a man, the crowd's hero,
>
> Que toutes mes hontes j'eus bues.
> I would be double,
> Half lover-poet-sybil,
> Half what the kind nets swallow....

Did I want to be a man? Not that I can remember, certainly not sexually. But I must have thought that "To be a man, the crowd's hero" was what becoming a published poet would mean; it was where my ambition was driving me. Then the definition changes to something female but disturbing: "Half lover-poet-sybil." How could you be a sybil by halves? I recognized, though I still did not fully recognize, the doubleness of my urge to become. What was expected of me, what I wanted for myself in the most profound ways, was marriage and children. I saw the "nets" as "kind," even though they were also the "coils" of my middle-class heritage. (And I was still living at home.) I didn't really think you could be double. At the University of Iowa, some years later, a classmate told me he believed that to be a woman poet was "a contradiction in terms." But by then I had gone back to writing, and for keeps.

a poem with capital letters

john berryman asked me to write a poem about roosters.
elizabeth bishop, he said, once wrote a poem about roosters.

do your poems use capital letters? he asked. *like god?*
i said. *god no,* he said, *like princeton!* i said,
god preserve me if i ever write a poem about princeton,
     and i thought,
o john berryman, what has brought me into this company
     of poets
where the masculine thing to do is use capital letters
and even princeton struts like one of god's betters?

There is something in this rhyme that even today brings
back the rollicking fall afternoon when Berryman, then a
young instructor and no more than a campus acquaintance,
rushed across the college lawn and, without even pausing
to say hello, began to tell me how to write my poems! Not
because of what it says (I recorded the conversation almost
in its entirety) but because it catches some of the laughter
yet also bewilderment I felt at "the company of poets,"
where "the masculine thing to do," etc.

Princeton truly was a male stronghold in those days, and
no doubt this intensified my own sense of a dichotomy
between "woman" and "poet." I knew a number of men
who wrote but no women. Work by women was still only
sparsely represented in contemporary poetry anthologies.
Now that I have a number of women friends who are poets,
it's hard to recall the particular kind of isolation I felt in my
writing or my almost beleaguered self-questioning.

I do remember how, when I was about fourteen, my sister
had brought home from Vassar Muriel Rukeyser's first two
books and I had a sudden glimpse of a young woman, not
much older than my sister, who was out in the world
writing poems; it seemed a life of extraordinary courage. I
continued to hear about Rukeyser from time to time. Other-
wise, men's praise of women poets didn't seem to go much
beyond Marianne Moore and Elizabeth Bishop, whose work
I admired but couldn't then use, in the deep sense that
writers use the discoveries of other writers as steps toward
their own growth. Somehow I had absorbed out of the New
Critical air itself (because I honestly don't remember any-
one's telling me so) that women have trouble managing
traditional meters with authority and verve and also can't

31

handle long lines. Emily Dickinson's lines were short, and besides, since I knew only the bowdlerized, smoothed-over versions of her poems, it didn't occur to me how original she could be musically within those repeated New England hymn tunes. So I went to school to what models I could find—mostly the British poets already mentioned—to learn long rhythmic periods and metrical invention within the forms. The subjects I was writing about—war and relations between women and men—seemed also mostly to have remained the property of men.

I'm afraid it is typical—the year was still only 1948— that I was at my most "literary" when I wrote a loose theme-and-variations using characters from *The Tempest* as voices for my own deep-seated fears:

Prospero:
> Health is what I have to buy for my children.
> If I ransom grace, that dream of prows and discovery
> And all except a physical creation,
> Do you think I can have it? will the stirrings of the air let me?

Miranda:
> O sweet Ariel, sweet strings who play with the idea of pain
> Not feeling it, who don't take in the cost
> Of following music suffered by the brain
> And not the blood, can't you hear the sailors cry *All's lost!*

That first line was, I know, meant quite literally. I was concerned for my unborn children if I persisted in being a writer, not primarily devoted to "a physical creation." Never very strong, I questioned whether I would have the energy to be a good mother unless I gave up other options.

The second stanza is still more complicated. For the old worry that to write might mean to wait on the sidelines, not really to act and suffer and "exist," which was present in the poems about wartime as guilt at nonparticipation, was now beginning to be metamorphosed into a conflict between writing and my own sexuality. Here, as Miranda follows "music suffered by the brain / And not the blood," it is the "sailors" who cry *All's lost!* In a very early poem I had written "Everyone's childhood lies buried in the sea."

Several years later, in the poem "Meteors," I was to make the farseeing, less physical (as I thought then) artist-lover into the "aviator," who suffers only in imagination as he bombs, while the "sailor," the lover who promises sexual and family satisfaction, lies mired in his very physicality. Almost half *Mercator's World*, and in particular the poems of 1949 and 1950, explore, on the one hand, the dilemma of a woman artist in love with a man who is not an artist and who therefore can't altogether share her cravings ("Could you construct a me / All physical reality?") and, on the other hand, the dilemma of one in love with a fellow artist ("I still remember evenings when I learned / The tricks of style..."). In a poem finished just before I stopped writing, "In a Room with Picassos," the woman artist is questioning not only the male artist but the tools of her own art, that is, the morality of her creative impulse.

Even that 1947 poem about "the archipelago of love," written out of all my dazzled awareness of the possibilities ahead of me and called "Design for an Odyssey," ends

> But perhaps our gods are weak, those islands useless

> Where they lie bright-eyed on the field of our illusion,
> White and flat like a fleet of summer boats.
> Suppose they are really too small and we sail alone
> Past the antipodes of desire and doubt?

Questions of Autobiography

But poetry isn't autobiography, and if some of the poems I've quoted from here most extensively were more successful, I probably wouldn't use them in the same way. For what poetry must do is alert us to a truth, and it must be necessary; once it exists, we realize how much we needed exactly this. Writing about the war was important for me personally, but I didn't, couldn't have much to say about it that could be fresh for others—as, for instance, Dylan Thomas's "A Refusal to Mourn" and "Holy Spring" had brought me up short when I first read them in the little book *Deaths and Entrances*, standing in a London bookstall,

33

wondering if I could afford to buy. In the end, my book was never "a book of war poems from a woman's point of view," for the reason that the real discoveries I was making in those days were being documented in the poems about man-woman relationships, which nevertheless depended on a lot of the same imagery. The most truthful poem I was to write about World War II—the elegy called "The Faithful"—didn't come along until 1955, ten years after the fact. There the point is not so much the narrator's grief (real enough) as her realization that her "blameless" life has been a kind of not living. I finally wrote my poem about being a nonparticipant, about the guilt of that, and I found after this country had been in Viet Nam for almost ten years that the poem took on new meaning and was again just as valid for me, and valid to be read aloud, as it had seemed originally.

A poem uses everything we know, the surprising things we notice, whatever we can't solve that keeps on growing, but it has to reach beyond autobiography even to stay on the page. Autobiography is not true enough; it has to be rearranged to release its full meaning. What I see in the poems that now go under the title "Mercator's World" is a rapid wearing-away of assumptions about what a love relationship should and can be between two people. At the time I was writing some of the later poems, these truths seemed terrible. In an early 1950s journal I find the note: "Perhaps I am afraid to write [because]:...I might kill some comfortable acceptance of myself in the minds of other people, or even in my own mind." Adrienne Rich has spoken of the need of women writers to be *nice*. The "you" of the poems is a projection of any one of three men (not who they were but the archetypes I made of them), but also, of course, there are poems in which the "you" is imaginary, like "Long View from the Suburbs," where, at least partly, I was trying to invent how it might feel to be the old Maud Gonne, whose extraordinary photographs had appeared in *Life* magazine. The rhetoric remains heavy (that need to write long lines, to have a battery of sound-effects at my command—like a man?), but, at best, the passion speaks

34

through its frames. In cutting eighty-odd poems down to a dozen, in the end I've wanted to keep only two of the "war" poems: "For a Boy Born in Wartime" and "After the Bomb Tests." In any case, by 1951 the war had begun to seem like a mask, something to write *through* in order to express a desolation that had become personal:

> Guilt, war, disease—pillars of violence
> To keep a roof of symbols over my head.
> Still the rain soaks my bed
> Whenever the wind blows, riddling innocence.
> A few survive
> By the effort of some individual love.

Is this what I thought, that only through an individual relationship could there be any real survival? By then, or anyway by a year afterward, with a record of three failed "efforts" inside five years, my chances must have seemed pretty slim.

Why Didn't I Publish?

Why, then, didn't I publish? And why, even more, did I give up writing poems, and when I went back to poems eventually change my style, after I'd worked so hard to make myself into a certain kind of poet during five crucially formative years? In fact, by the winter of 1951-52, it felt almost more as if poetry had given me up.

I think it is important to ask these questions just because I didn't give up poetry for marriage, or to have a baby, or because the family washing was getting hopelessly ahead of me. Maybe I gave it up, or put it to one side, precisely because I still hoped for those things. If this seems cowardly: "Didn't anyone ever tell you it was all right to write?" asked the psychiatrist who came along much later. "Yes, but not to be a writer." Behind me lay the sort of upper-middle-class education that encourages writing, painting, music, theater so long as they aren't taken too seriously, so long as they can be set aside once the real business of life begins.

35

(But aren't men often blocked in just these same ways?) I had no women models, as we now understand that word— and that need. I didn't even know many older women who worked. Not only my parents but I myself consciously wanted me to marry and have children. Physical energy was limited. I write slowly. It was the era of *The Feminine Mystique*. And it seems to me even now that the difficulties we all sensed and continue to sense are real and to be respected. I saw clearly how hard it would be for me to make a lasting relationship, bring up children and "live a full life as a woman," while being a committed writer. The women poets I read about were generally not known for their rich, stable sexual and family lives.

Such problems must have faced any young woman of my age who thought of being a poet. Beyond this, each of us can only speak for the problems of her own temperament and her own personal history. As I've already suggested, I was both quite conservative socially at this period and becoming radical in my insights. "Half lover-poet-sybil / Half what the kind nets swallow." An impossible combination. When I first reread the old poems, I was struck by the number that use *seeing* as a metaphor. Seeing equals truth-telling. I wanted to see far, like an astronomer, and I wanted to see through, as if by X-rays. But "The urge to tell the truth / Strips sensuality." Domesticity, too. If the poems have a virtue that makes some of them worth printing even after all these years, despite their immaturities, despite a blocky, half-borrowed rhetorical style, I think it is not only as a historical record but because of their psychological acuteness. At the same time, a woman painter to whom I showed them not long ago commented on how persistently they seek the "bone," how only the very last, "Obligations," has any concern for human "breathing." There is a kind of corrosive perfectionism running throughout—a perfection-ism that made me end "The Door," in its final draft, with a bid for transcendent union, using an image of X-rays for the recognition at zero-level I wanted the lovers to achieve, while another poem about an almost paralyzed affair, "Twins," uses X-rays as an image of destructive knowing.

36

I can't say I didn't recognize how much, if I gave up poetry, I'd be giving up:

> Foresee me now huddled in my kitchen
> Like the woman Ronsard wrote to, shelling peas,
> Slag-haired, grained like a rock in the Atlantic,
> Having survived the age for lovers and
> All subsequent ages, married to the bone
> In Greenland....

suggests a marriage which, in its dedication to things of the earth and away from poetry, "will destroy me." "Washing across my face / Look where they drag and scar—the peas, the children." But the truth is, I had come to view poetry as even more destructive. I seemed to have made a mess of my most intimate friendships, and poetry—that gift for seeing far and seeing through—now looked less like a source of renewal (as it had at Oxford) than the house-wrecker. By the winter of 1950-51, though I was still often writing well, I was beginning to be appalled by the images of "guilt, war, disease" that dominated my thinking and kept appearing in the poems almost in spite of myself. Poems like "Meteors" and "After the Bomb Tests" (where Kepler becomes the "virgin artist" and the atomic-bomb explosion mimics human conception and birth) were mirrors into which I couldn't bear to gaze for long.

Teaching

"I see, you had to survive," said a wise friend recently, rather quickly laying the old manuscript aside. And indeed, as much as one can by an act of will, I set about to change my life. In September of 1950 I left Princeton to go into teaching, something I had believed in humanly since that summer at Oxford but had kept putting off. I started in at once at Sarah Lawrence College, which was more, with only a B.A. and no previous experience, than I deserved. I remember that during one of my interviews I was asked, "And why do you think you can teach poetry?" and I answered, "Because it's the one place where I'd as soon take my own word as anybody else's," though I went on to explain that that didn't mean I thought I was always right! Still, it was eight years before I was given a poetry course. I taught fiction and fiction writing, and to women students. In place of the part-time freelance editing job I was used to, which had left me with free mornings and plenty of free-floating fantasy out of which to write, I was soon working sixty hours a week. I cared very much about those students, and there was everything to learn.

The poems of 1950-51, that first teaching winter, are curiously mixed. I was able to finish several of my angriest Princeton pieces, like "Twins" and "Long View from the Suburbs." I wrote several ambitious new poems ("After the Bomb Tests" started out to be a sonnet-ring) in the old style. At the same time, I was beginning to loosen up, to want to use more natural imagery, but also not to be able to develop all I wrote in the old decisive way. This led to its own kind of despair. I didn't yet want poetry to sound like conversation, but the rhetoric I'd been accustomed to and had tried so hard to perfect ("Head first, face down, into Mercator's world") seemed altogether out of keeping with the life I was now leading. I wrote some rather sweet, static poems about children, landscapes, old men. I don't even remember writing "In a Room with Picassos," where not only the fellow artist but my own role as artist was put to the test. The most satisfying challenge of the year was "Obligations," which later seemed like the last of the old and first of the new—the only poem of the early group to find its way, in somewhat revised form, into my 1969 book. It was the last of the old in that I remember working out the structure quite carefully as a series of abstract geometric figures (the circle that reduces itself to a point, then is opened out again by the "broken shining blade"), which are also of course sexual analogies; but it is also quite an honest poem about an accepted human encounter, with its own built-in griefs, and it is set in a stubble field, by daylight, with real insects humming, rather than against some hallucinated sky or sea. One version makes the sexual tie "our defense, which we shall soon evade"; another, the one I have used here because it seems to be the one I came back to, calls it "our defense, which we cannot evade." It was still a time of uncertainty for me, even crisis.

Otto Rank suggested to Anaïs Nin that women have trouble being artists because they damp down what is destructive in them, therefore they can't create freely either. Nin concludes, "In order to create without destroying, I nearly destroyed myself." By the end of 1951, my awareness of crisis had in fact reached a peak. I who had started out asking for equality with the men I knew now wondered whether I had been "castrating." I had a continual, grinding sense of loss and self-betrayal, which only the daily human wear-and-tear of teaching helped somewhat to offset if not change. It was during this second teaching winter that, almost more than my giving up poems, the poems seemed to give me up. What few I wrote were pale and diffuse, or full of self-pity. When I rewrote, I often blurred earlier insights. I was overworked, my health suffered, above all I wanted to learn how to live. By the time I had gone back to writing and, in 1957, was beginning to publish in magazines, I didn't even want to look back at that first manuscript. I remembered it as more destructive than it could ever possibly have been.

Is this primarily a political story, having to do with how hard it is for a woman to *feel* the freedom that would let her develop as a writer, even when she has it? Is it a tale of personal neurosis? Or is it simply the history of one individual woman, probably more twisted than I've allowed for here by lovers' claims and family ambitions, in which—as in any history—accident too played a part, but whose echoes may reverberate? For we need all the connections we can make.

> En l'an trentiesme de mon aage
> Perhaps I shall discover
> That each is coward other
> And drinking shame, creep into time's cage.

ends the birthday poem I wrote at twenty-three, though it

was an ending I was never really satisfied with. Maybe, I was saying, instead of feeling "wiser" and more secure by the time I reached thirty, I'd find out instead that to be either "lover-poet-sybil" or a housewife would be a kind of cowardice, because I couldn't be both. Since each would be only a half-life, maybe they would add up to the same life? The final "cage" might not be a matter of choice at all but the necessary compromises of aging, of facing myself. Even then I had the foretaste of shame, like a numbing drug.

A Room of My Own, with Windows

I have said that I gave up poetry, but after all it seems as if I never quite gave up the idea of writing. To have been convinced for so long that I gave it up altogether may have been the last deception I practiced on myself in connection with that early work, those early years. For I still have the journal I kept during the winter and spring of 1952-53, the year before I went to the University of Iowa to (as I told everybody) observe teaching methods at the Writers' Workshop there. I hadn't been at Iowa more than three or four weeks before I was deep in stories of my own and, once more, poems. By the second semester the stories had been laid aside.... But what the journal documents is that it was started deliberately as a way of getting me back to writing, through the sanity of observed detail, and that I had begun to think seriously about fiction. Fiction might prove a more humane mode than poetry. Did I also have some idea (the journal doesn't say so) that to be a woman short-story writer might be more acceptable than being a woman poet?

Most of all I wanted to get people into what I wrote— people who were not mere projections of my own needs and angers but people walking around and talking, recognizably *other*, as unique and often funny as my students had turned out to be. If seeing was the metaphor for truth-telling in the poems that lay just behind me, seeing from the height of an airplane or with the intensity of X-rays, then looking was what I aimed for by 1953, truly looking at the world around me and trying to record it. I was touched by Ransom's notion that it is the specific detail, intimately rendered, that reveals our love for a subject. Much of the journal is simply notes I took out my New York City windows. In the fall of 1952 I had moved to a walk-up on West Sixteenth Street, between Seventh and Eighth Avenues, and this neighborhood was shocking me awake in a new way. In my mind was that room I always remember, again from the summer of 1947, in heavily shelled St. Mâlo: *Two walls of an old stone building are still standing, up one of which climbs a bare stone staircase. Halfway up, pitched over space and rubble, is cantilevered a brand-new timber box—yellow, fresh-smelling, inhabited—with a potted red geranium in its one immaculate window-square.*

For despite my memory of the strain of those years, the journal is honest, strong, feeling, and it even has a kind of natural gaiety. It speaks of the necessity for changing myself, for finding a new style both of being and writing, to go with the changed realities I now perceived. It explores what might be required for short stories and outlines a good many plots. Because the mechanistic imagery I had used so far had begun to horrify me, and certainly contradicted in intent and almost in coloration what I wanted to do next, it suggests that a new imagery must be found, less like a crustacean's shell. But to change one's images is like trying to revolutionize one's dreams. It can't be done overnight. Nor can it be effected by will. I find one entry reading: "Something seems to have broken in me last year, like a spring breaking....What broke...is perhaps the sense that you can build your life by choice. Now I think you build it out of necessities—and that all you can do is answer these necessities in the decentest way possible....I am trying to learn to lead a decent life and not want to be a great person and, at the same time, know what I have the human right to draw the line at."

"Not want to be a great person." ("To be a man, the crowd's hero.") I was jolted when I discovered those words written out, for how rarely we admit we want to be great persons. Women's needs to appear modest, certainly my own need, is almost as powerful as the need to be "nice," and no doubt not at all separate from it.

The journal gives specific reasons for the failure of the poems of the previous five years and even of my whole concept of poetry. Too "musical," for one thing. "I think first of all in terms of a very definite rhythm and structure. Emotionally, too, I think in terms of rhetoric, of an impassioned dramatization of a moment....Now I can no longer capture those moods...and so the whole rhetorical machinery seems...out of date. My poetry was heroic poetry, and now what I have to say doesn't concern heroes, and I haven't the heart to change the machinery, taking out a screw here and a blade there, to make it something different, and less, than it was....The poetry I have written this year is just empty mechanics or else it hardly comes into being."

Again: "I have a very old-fashioned idea of what poetry should do. It is the soul's history and whatever troubles the soul is fit material for poetry. Therefore I was right to try to write war poems, even if they were often overblown, because no one can live just personally, just observing the workings of his own consciousness, these days. Now I am trying to write [about] love—but giving the quality of the other person."

And finally: "To begin with, love is a joyful recognition of capacities within yourself. It is yourself you fall in love with. Much later, perhaps, the individual with whom you are in love comes to mean more than the condition of 'being in love.' For some people this means a comedown to what they call friendship; for others, it is marriage....The first abstract stage is the stage of poetry. Does the second stage imply fiction, or just a different kind of poetry, a poetry of development rather than passionate lyrical statement?"

How much one would like to be able to argue with one's younger self! And yet was this concept of poetry—that it should be heroic, "musical" (i.e., romantically metrical, with "a very definite rhythm and structure"), and even abstract—so different from that other concept, which I'd been brought up to and wanted to believe, that I should find the *solution* to my life, not just companionship, in a single, other person? (And that I still wanted marriage, the imagery of the last paragraph makes perfectly clear.) The final version of "The Door" showed what a weight this put on the men I knew, as well as on myself. They had to be heroic, and not the least of my mistakes lay in blaming myself when it turned out, humanly enough, to be otherwise.

But most of the journal is not so didactic, nor even particularly meditative. I was living on a half-Irish, half-Puerto Rican block, and I wrote about the boys burning Christmas greens in the gutters in January; about the soft-drink bar where the older boys hung out, smoking, perched on orange crates along the sidewalk, almost under the lee of a crumbling brownstone called "Rainbow"; I recorded the little girls' street games and some of their chants. One day in May an amusement truck came along, shaped like a gigantic popcorn popper with loudspeakers on top, and as the children were jounced down and then up almost to the height of the first-story windows, one cried, "Hey, look at the sky!". From my fire escape I made a rough sketch of the truck body, with approximate dimensions. I thought of the windows across the street from mine as eye-pairs, two to a family, into which I could look and which would sometimes stare back at me out of their separate, never-fully-to-be-understood worlds.

An Art of the Unexpected

My getting back to poems again, the following year, is really another story. I think I am still trying to work out a "poetry of development." And certainly when I first started at Iowa I had to face the embarrassment (to call it by a mild name) of knowing that what I wrote was far weaker, from any standpoint but my own, than what I had been doing three or four years before. It was after all not just a matter of "taking out a screw here and a blade there, to make... something different." My whole intention as a writer had changed. In trying for a more generous habit of mind, for

43

instance, whether deliberately or not I set aside the kind of anger that often goes along with sexuality as one of the pivots of my work. I wonder how many women share with me this history, of not having wanted to admit their anger? I did write as an observer, almost too patiently. For a while children, landscapes, old men predominated. It is very difficult to practice any art wholeheartedly and not to compromise, at least now and then, teaching as well as maternal roles, community responsibility. There is the danger of self-centeredness, if not downright selfishness. On the other hand, for writers especially, just because they use words, it is hard to be generous and never to indulge in self-censorship.

These questions that confront women writers (and of course, many men too) are, far more than the questions I opened with, the ones that continue to trouble me. How are we to balance our needs? It's unlikely that any young woman poet today would simply suppress her work, as I did. And I wish I hadn't. Yet I can't be sorry that *The Weather of Six Mornings*, when it finally appeared, was based on certain rather broad human acceptances. I had to get through the perfectionism of those early poems, to learn that no choice is absolute and no structure can save us. If I no longer hesitate to bring out a few pages from that first manuscript, the questions are just as urgent as they ever were. All the more reason, I think, to accept as part of whatever I now am that young, cabined, often arrogant, but questing and vivid self whose banishment I've come to recognize as one more mistaken absolute. For if my poems have always been about survival— and I believe they have been—then survival too keeps revealing itself as an art of the unexpected.

New York, 1974

3
The Weather of Six Mornings

1954-1965

Morning on the St. John's

The Chinese character for landscape is
mountains-and-water. A Japanese image
of heaven is Fuji reflected in a pool.

This is a country where there are no mountains:
At dawn the water birds like lines of rain
Rise from the penciled grasses by the river
And slantwise creak across the growing light.
The sky lifts upward and the breath of flowers
Wakes with the shadows of the waking birds.

The shadows of the birds, the dancing birds!
With so much freedom who could ask for mountains?
The heron stands here ankle-deep in flowers,
Wet hyacinths that burn more blue with rain,
And waves of smaller wings hurl wide the light
All up and down the horizontal river.

And now the sun shakes blue locks in the river
And rises dripping-headed while the birds
Go wild in curves of praise at sudden light.
The fire that would flash instantly off mountains
Bathes this round world in dew as dark as rain
And then strikes green and gold among the flowers.

The dropping heads, the smooth and shaken flowers!
(Among the grasses, blue eyes by the river,
And in the garden, fires after rain.)
Under umbrella leaves the mockingbirds
Still nestle and trill quietly of mountains,
Then whistle Light!—cadenza—Light! and Light!

While higher and higher sweeps the opening light
In bluish petals as of opening flowers,
More pure than snow at dawn among the mountains.
Paler than any flush along the river,

Beyond the reach of eyefall flight of birds,
It floods a sky swept innocent by rain.

The assault of sun, the long assault of rain—
Look how our darkness is made true by light!
Look how our silence is confirmed by birds!
The mind that pastured ankle-deep in flowers
Last night, must wake to sunrise on the river,
Graze wide and then grow vertical as mountains;

For even a glimpse of mountains fogged with rain
Or mirrored in a river brings delight
And shakes us all as dawn shakes birds and flowers.

Jacksonville, Florida

Leaving Water Hyacinths

from an old photograph, Jacksonville, 1933

I see you, child, standing above the river
Like a thin bush, too young for bloom or fruit
But solidly planted, both knees locked backward
And blue-gray eyes quietly, typically watchful:
The catboats play over a chuckling sunlight
(Funny how waves slide over, sunlight under!)
And hyacinths grip down, rooted in heaven.

I know—because you become me—you say goodbye
To thumping dark paddle-like hyacinth leaves
With blood-brown stems and blue and sucking heads,
To the river's massive purr, its sustained dredge
And flap at the dock stilts (stiff, a heron's legs)—
Sounds which can stop in air your breakfast teaspoon
Or lap as lights across the bedtime ceiling.

I know—because you contain me—you seem cool-eyed
And yet you sense that once you leave this landing
Your whole life after will be sailing back:
A seeking out of losses, the catboats' débris
Which cloud a harbor but bloom upward blue,
And where the heron climbs, his lank limbs dropping,
Music that cradles grief to an Atlantic.

For My Mother in Her First Illness, from a Window Overlooking Notre Dame

Why can I never when I think about it
See your face tender under the tasseled light
Above a book held in your stubby fingers?
Or catch your tumbling gamecock angers?
Or—as a child once, feverish by night—
Wake to your sleepless, profiled granite?

But I must reconstruct you, feature by feature:
Your sailor's gaze, a visionary blue,
Not stay-at-home but wistful northern eyes;
And the nose Gothic, oversized,
Delicately groined to the eyesockets' shadow,
Proud as a precipice above laughter.

Arrogant as a cathedral or the sea
You carry your blue spaces high and quick
On a young step, tapping or chivalrous.
Pilgrim of the ridiculous
And of a beauty now almost archaic,
I miss your swift inward, your needle's eye.

Light stalk, my love is all of movement,
Those ribs of quicksand feeling in your face,
Those knowledgeable, energetic gargoyles.
Still haunted by my first devils,
Alone and sick, lying in a foreign house,
I try to read. Which one of us is absent?

The Faithful

Once you said joking slyly, *If I'm killed*
I'll come to haunt your solemn bed,
I'll stand and glower at the head
And see if my place is empty still, or filled.

What was it woke me in the early darkness
Before the first bird's twittering?
—A shape dissolving and flittering
Unsteady as a flame in a drafty house.

It seemed a concentration of the dark burning
By the bedpost at my right hand
While to my left that no man's land
Of sheet stretched palely as a false morning....

All day I have been sick and restless. This evening
Curtained, with all the lights on,
I start up—only to sit down.
Why should I grieve after ten years of grieving?

What if last night I was the one who lay dead
While the dead burned beside me
Trembling with passionate pity
At my blameless life and shaking its flamelike head?

Bermuda

Old man, step out in the sun,
The white blind of one o'clock!
Across the road a rusty cock
Stalks, his wars forgotten.

Here red and purple hang
From trees and tropic sky,
A cockscomb sunblaze, high—
Or the rains clang

On tin roof and gutterspout
And hot palms whistling.
Old man, stop rustling
Your shaking plumes, step out!

Rock Climbing

Higher than gulls' nests, higher than children go,
Scrambling and dangling to survey the sea,
    We crest the last outcropping strewn
        East of this island.

Now pell-mell, now stopping to pinch a finger
In an open fissure down which no sun glints,
    Where water gnaws and subsides, we comb
        As the tide rises

Each rock that locks us in a partial vision
Of the expanding, curved and eye-reflecting blue
    Which liberates but still hangs over
        Our minds' breathing.

As yet the gleams are steep and unexpected:
We study lichens like a dying scale,
    Silver as fishes; here crisp moss
        Moist in a crevice;

Then even lichens powder, and the rocks
Give way to sunny tables, dry escarpments,
    Each with its different texture, pocked
        Or smoothly sloping

Down to the pitch where barnacles or stain
Dark as a rust line show the heaving power
    Of water's shoulders, raised at night,
        Then wrested over.

And now the last rock! piled hugely up
And shoved to end a sprinkle like a jetty
    Of little boulders in the green-brown
        Irregular surface

Where seaweed shaped like coral swimming, kelp,
Pebbles and broken shells of clam or crab
   All shine or flicker up as down-watching
      We kneel and wonder.

Now balancing, laughing, brisk as children who
Spread out their arms and toe along a pole
   We skip from top to top, lift knees,
      Come out at angles

Until we have scaled it! stand aloft at last
With all the ocean for our freedom and
   Our meditation, all the swing
      Of limbs for glitter.

Warmed by the sun, tingling, with tired calves
And eyes of exultation we address
   The father of our knowledge, shrouded
      Faintly beyond us

At the lost line where wind is turned to water
And all is turned to light, dissolved or rinsed
   To silver where our eyes fish (gulls
      Sailing and falling

Out, out....) And now the seabirds call
Far off, recalled by memories like hunger,
   Screech and return, flying the tides
      Of pure air inward

To where their nests are, intimate and cold;
While standing on those cliffs we slowly rest
   And looking back to hillsides build
      Imaginary houses.

Deer Isle, Maine

The Builder of Houses

What was the blond child building
Down by the pond at near-dark
When the trees had lost their gilding
And the giant shadows stepped
To the water's edge, then stopped?
With intent fingers, doing a boy's work
In a boy's old sweater,
She hammered against her dear world's dirty weather.

Proud of her first house
Which boasted an orange-crate ceiling,
A pillow, a stuffed mouse,
And room for complete privacy
In the obvious crotch of a tree,
She skipped and swagged; rude cousins came stealing
With boys' laughter
And dismantled all but one branchy rafter.

She hunted almost till summer
Before her second find:
A post like a sunken swimmer
Deep in the marsh where ducks
Made nesting clucks and squawks.
With cautious tappings she fashioned a duck blind—
Or so her stepfather
Claimed when his autumn guns began to gather.

All winter in secret mourning
She toiled on her third house.
Three miles from the driveway turning
Up a forgotten path,
Risking her mother's wrath,
She tramped until her footprints filled with ice.
That bright glazing
Revealed one day her high and forbidden blazing.

In the very swaying top
Of a windswept sugar maple
She had built a bare prop—
Five boards to hold the crouch
Of a fugitive from search.
Here on this slippery and hard-won table,
Armed with her hammer,
She was tracked down by dogs' and parents' clamor.

There was only one more trial:
When frozen, brackish March
Gave way to floods in April
She rowed a sadly leaking
Scow, its oarlocks creaking,
Out to an island in the glittering reach,
And there, halfheartedly,
Began to floor the bend of a stunted tree.

Why was this last, diminished
And never-mentioned mansion
The one she never could finish?
No one—not father nor mother
Nor even the mellowing weather—
Routed her from her chosen foothold and passion;
This time house and view
Were hers, island and vision to wander through.

But less and less she balanced
Her boat on the sunrise water
Or from her window glanced
To where that outline glimmered;
Island and house were inner,
And perhaps existed only for love to scatter
Such long, carefully planned
And sovereign childhood with its disrespectful hand.

Acceptances

1 | THE SUNDIAL

Take out of time that moment when you stood
On the far porch, a monolith of man,
And I raised one flag arm above my head:
Two statues crying out in shapes of stone.

And take that moment when your flame-blue eyes
Blazed on me till true sunlight seemed to fail
And all our landscape fell away like lies:
The burr of bees, grass, flowers, the slow sundial.

And take that moment after kneeling speech
—*Rare things must be respected*, your lips said—
When moveless I withheld myself from reach,
Unmoving, gave my need to fill your need.

Behind us in the garden the great sundial
Began to stretch its shadow toward afternoon.
Nothing was altered. Only we sat still,
Spent with sane joy beyond the bees' numb drone.

2 | THE GRAVEYARD

Where five old graves lay circled on a hill
And pines kept all but shattered sunlight out
We came to learn about
How each had sinned, loved, suffered, lost until
He met the other and grew somehow still.

Under those soughing, rumor-speaking trees
Full of dead secrets, on the August ground,
We leaned against a mound
Not touching; there, as we could, gave keys
To open midnight vaults that no one sees.

All that had shaped us thirty years or more
We tried to offer—not as brave youngsters do
Who need an echo, who
See in their fathers' sins a canceled score—
But as two grieving inmates tapping at the door.

Gifts of the self which were but bids for power,
Gifts of the innocent self—stripped, bound and torn—
A rare child wrongly born
And our best strivings turned, with age, half-sour:
Such darkness we unlocked within an hour.

Those five old graves lay speechless while the sun
Gradually stroked them with its flickering arm.
The smell of pines grew warm.
We walked away to watch a fresh stream run
As free as if all guilts were closed and done.

3 | THE RACETRACK

Under our stillness fled the same low hooves—
After, before, from the first morning when
We stood to watch the horses exercise.
Like a small sea the track dazzled our eyes:
Two riders shouting, flattening to run,
A spray of turf flung glistening toward the sun,
Stallions and fillies combing like distant waves.

Blind, pounding beasts came whirling through the mist,
Sweat on their flanks, their ankles wreathed in spume,
The day I told you of my loneliness;
Or I saw darkly out of such distress
As knocked my heart against its fragile room
Until our eyes touched and that light went home—
So we were one before we spoke or kissed.

Now that our bodies move and wake as one
That daybreak dream of horses has changed too
And we are free to say, as shadows scatter,
Sound carries on this track as on deep water.
The trees shake out their leaves. We feel the slow
Rotation of a world in which we grow;
Slowly we learn our long wave's luminous motion.

In the Last Few Moments Came
the Old German Cleaning Woman

Our last morning in that long room,
Our little world, I could not cry
But went about the Sunday chores
—Coffee and eggs and newspapers—
As if your plane would never fly,
As if we were stopped there for all time.

Wanting to fix by ritual
The marriage we could never share
I creaked to stove and back again.
Leaves in the stiffening New York sun
Clattered like plates; the sky was bare—
I tripped and let your full cup fall.

Coffee scalded your wrist and that
Was the first natural grief we knew.
Others followed after years:
Dry fodder swallowed, then the tears
When mop in hand the old world through
The door pressed, dutiful, idiot.

A Little Vesper

Another day gone, and still
I haven't answered those letters
that clog my desk and heart.
The sky is a blown-up page
scribbled by swallows; the sun
drops in a pearl of mist
under an orange roof—
What am I hankering for?

Idly I hum this poem
as I wait for the tiny shriek
of a swallow outside, the whistle
of a leaf on my dry porch.
Sometimes it rains here. Letters
are piled up now like old snow
in the cramp of the spring evening—
Everyone sends their love.

And what do I want, ever,
more than these simple names
crying solicitude
from a black scrawl, beyond seas?
Swallows, it's time to fly home,
crawl in under the tiles
and bed with what we are—
breathe goodnight to the first strangers.

Rome

In the House of the Dying

So once again, hearing the tired aunts
whisper together under the kitchen globe,
I turn away; I am not one of them.

At the sink I watch the water cover my hands
in a sheath of light. Upstairs she lies alone
dreaming of autumn nights when her children were born.

On the steps between us grows in a hush of waiting
the impossible silence between two generations.
The aunts buzz on like flies around a bulb.

I am dressed like them. Standing with my back turned
I wash the dishes in the same easy way.
Only at birth and death do I utterly fail.

For death is my old friend who waits on the stairs.
Whenever I pass I nod to him like the newsman
who is there every day; for them he is the priest.

While the birth of love is so terrible to me
I feel unworthy of the commonest marriage.
Upstairs she lies, washed through by the two miracles.

My Young Mother

My young mother, her face narrow
and dark with unresolved wishes
under a hatbrim of the twenties,
stood by my middleaged bed.

Still as a child pretending sleep
to a grownup watchful or calling,
I lay in a corner of my dream
staring at the mole above her lip.

Familiar mole! but that girlish look
as if I had nothing to give her—
Eyes blue—brim dark—
calling me from sleep after decades.

Letters

1

That quiet point of light
trembled and went out.

Iron touches a log:
it crumbles to coal, then ashes.

The log sleeps in its shape.
A new moon rises.

Darling, my white body
still bears your imprint.

2

Autumn has come
in early July.

Outside three crows
make their harsh, rainy scraping.

On the ground white petals:
my rain-soaked letters.

The Weather of Six Mornings

1

Sunlight lies along my table
like abandoned pages.

I try to speak
of what is so hard for me

—this clutter of a life—
Puritanical signature!

In the prolonged heat insects,
pine needles, birch leaves

make a ground bass of silence
that never quite dies.

2

Treetops are shuddering
in uneasy clusters

like rocking water
whirlpooled before a storm.

Words knock at my breast,
heave and struggle to get out.

A black-capped bird
pecks on, unafraid.

Yield then, yield
to the invading rustle of the rain!

3

All is closed in
by an air so rain-drenched

the distant barking of tied-up dogs
ripples to the heart of the woods.

Only a man's voice
refuses to be absorbed.

Hearing of your death
by a distant roadside

I wanted to erect some marker
though your ashes float out to sea.

4

If the weather breaks
I can speak of your dying,

if the weather breaks,
if the crows stop calling

and flying low
(again today there is thunder, out-

lying...),
I can speak of your living,

the lightning-flash of meeting,
the green leaves waving at our windows.

5

Yesterday a letter
spoke of our parting—

a kind of dissolution
so unlike this sudden stoppage.

Now all the years in between
flutter away like lost poems.

And the morning light is so delicate,
so utterly empty....

at high altitude, after long illness,
breathing in mote by mote a vanished world....

6

Rest.
A violin bow, a breeze

just touches the birches.
Cheep—a new flute

tunes up in a birch top.
A chipmunk's warning skirrs....

Whose foot disturbs these twigs?
To the sea of received silence

why should I sign
my name?

4
March

A Sequence

1967

March

1 | FEATHERS

I've died, but you are still living!
The pines are still living, and the eastern sky.
Today a great bustle rocks the treetops
of snow and sunshine, dry branches, green brooms.

The pines are cleaning their attics.
Mercilessly, they lop off weak twigs.
If I look down from my window
I can see one of the walks we used to take together.

The snow is covered with brown feathers.
In the fields it's as if an army had just limped by
leaving its slight corpses, abandoned weapons—
a wreckage that will melt into spring.

Nearby is a little grove; on brown needles
we lay side by side telling each other stories.
Against the glass here, listen—
Nothing can stop the huzzah of the male wind!

2 | HUNGER MOON

The last full moon of February
stalks the fields; barbed wire casts a shadow.
Rising slowly, a beam moved toward the west
stealthily changing position

until now, in the small hours, across the snow
it advances on my pillow
to wake me, not rudely like the sun
but with the cocked gun of silence.

I am alone in a vast room
where a vain woman once slept.
The moon, in pale buckskins, crouches
on guard beside her bed.

Slowly the light wanes, the snow will melt
and all the fences thrum in the spring breeze
but not until that sleeper, trapped
in my body, turns and turns.

3 | EL SUEÑO DE LA RAZÓN

for C. in a mental hospital

Cousin, it's of you I always dream
as I walk these dislocated lawns
or compose a stanza under the Corot trees.

The music of my walking reconciles,
somewhat, the clipped but common ground
with the lost treetops' thunderous heads.

How they are always muttering in the still
afternoon. How they create
their own darkness under hottest sun.

They compose clouds or a sea
so far above us we can scarcely tell
why such a premonition brushes our cheeks.

Yet as I walk I scan
the woods for a girl's white figure
slipping away among the pines' thin shafts.

Hiding, she is hiding, and in your dreams
the poem's cleared spaces
barely hold out

against marching trees, this suddenly Turner sky.
Poor furious girl, our voices sound
alike (your nurse told me), discreet and gentle.

4 | BACK

I was prepared for places
as someone packs bags against hell,
practicing each jolt of memory
before I stumbled over it.

Secretly I rehearsed the stages
of our coming to know one another,
furnished each scene with trees,
even a phoebe calling.

So I preserved a wintry face
as I returned little by little
to the rooms where we slept, the closet
where you hung your worn raincoat.

But tonight it's all sham—
From her curtained alcove a woman
hums that aria of Purcell's
tentatively, sweetly:

Dido is pleading, Aeneas
blurs into her past, his future.
Again your eyes star
with salt as I choose my elegy.

5 | NO MORE ELEGIES

The sun is so bright on the snow
I'm out tramping in dark beach glasses.
A clump of leafless birches
steams against a dark blue sky.

Over there the yellow frame
of some new construction glints,
while the tips of those bushes are bloody
as if tomorrow, tomorrow would be Easter!

And a phoebe is calling, calling.
All the small birds come fluting from the pines:
No more elegies! no more elegies! Poor
fools—it's not even spring.

6 | IN SILENCE WHERE WE BREATHE

As a boy he was so silent
she raged like a gnat. Summer nights—

Summer nights he stood at his desk
wrapped in a wordless soprano.

Once he constructed a clipper ship
to scale from the *Century Dictionary*.

All May they ran barefoot
through the stinging southern streets.

The air was like mercury,
a heavy silver ball.

And the river stank of salt
and rotten magnolia candles

down the end of the block. Slot machines!
From their grandmother's veranda

she could hear the ring of life
start out through a swing door—

No one could tell such stories;
but he never cried, not once.

7 | MIDDLE AGE

At last it's still—a gray thaw.
Who ever saw a more sullen day?
On the porch, among patches of standing water,
a bluejay pecks at an uncovered seed.

It's not even raining. In the vanished night
a brief snow fell, dampening the paths.
The paths are brown with ashes—
or is it the first earth showing through?

The pines are like saints. I'm waiting—
oh, for some insight, some musical phrase,
for the voices of my friends,
for faint traffic noises from the far-off city,

for choruses, for a symphony orchestra,
for the screech of a subway train rounding a bend,
a baby's ah-ah-ah
or the rich, hesitant speech of students—

How amazing to be born! A few drops
of rain fling their stones into puddles,
and circles of light ride out
smashing the icy islands—

I can't hear their splash. I'm alert
only to dreams as the rain falls louder.
Each word, each history cracks open.
Only the miracle is real.

8 | CODA: SMOKE

An air of departures. Silences.
Again the pines are sheathed in a wet snow.
The chimney breathes its slow, transparent smoke.

Everything has been offered, nothing given.
Everything, not the first thing has been said.
After me who will sit here, patiently writing?

Words over a page: a slow smoke
scrolling across the sky what is unconsumed
by the deep, thunderous fires of the house—

An air of departures. Now the tall city
stoops to receive us, where we blur like snow
leaving behind a breath of loves and angers.

5
Reclaimed Poems

1954-1969

Blind Girl

I take your hand. I want to touch your eyes.
They are water-soft. I know. I could push them in.
Once a doll's eyes fell in before my fingers—
Instead of dropping tick-tock open and shut
They were cold holes like a poor frozen faucet.
Where does the water come from? I hear breathing.
Listen at the tap—you hear a kind of sobbing.

But your eyes have a panting kind of hush
And then a shudder like a huddled bird's
Lifting his neck-feathers in my two cupped hands.
That's the light in them, asking to get let out.
(Your lashes beat and beat against my fingers.)
And when we walk together, heat on my shoulders
Is soft as down, and that's a light called outside.

So seeing is something struggling to get out
To something like it, larger but more still,
And when you see, that must feel just like swimming.
I take your hand. There. Please let me hold you.
If I hold tight enough to your live fingers
It *must* work free. Oh, I could kill your eyes
Only to know a little more what sight is.

[1954]

After Fever

There the four doctors were, sitting in comical attitudes
Of concern, agitation, and one with a fatuous happiness
Was counting my pulse as if to clock the beatitudes,
And one, at the foot of the bed, began to undress.

Out of my chaste and senseless golden sphere
Have I come back for this (I thought) resurrection?
Have I braved oceans and climbed up all those stairs
To burst on a scene of such rackety imperfection?

I lay on my bed like a poverty-stricken prisoner
From a Daumier cartoon. I had my thermometer read.
I adored my red-faced judges for just what they were
While the laughter banged round and round in my
    teakettle head.

[1955]

Roman Dream

She-death, my green mother, you
climbed invisibly toward me
up the black stairwell. I heard
you scratch, scratch, moistening
your lips as I tucked my skirt
tighter, sitting on the top
step, American, waiting.

Waiting for you to pass I
felt no fear. Behind me red-
gold Rome, rooftop café, my
lover, his woman, flowers.... Cold
stroked my throat. I thought, *No
one will know, no one in Rome
will ever know to find me.*

[1961]

Messages

1

Ragged and thrashing
the road between me and the ocean—

I trip on stumps.
A gull flies over:

Guilt! guilt! your father is dying!
The woods are studded with poisonous berries.

How smooth they shine
red as tail-lights, inviting—

The roar of a cliff.
From the tip of this plunge of darkness

a few stars telegraph:
Go back. Or else welcome.

2

Approaching my life I am terrified.
Stars in the mud trip me up.

Terrified, I lug stone after stone
up the wide, foot-bruising ladder of night.

Stones in a ring can't define it:
Night. Lake. Mirror. Deep. Only

[1968-69]

All These Dreams

All these dreams: the dream of the mountain cabin
where five of us ate off the floor in a bower of pines;
the dream of the house without rooms
where light poured down through the roof on a circular
    stair
made of glass, and there was one blue rug;
the dream of the workshop where, unmarried and pregnant,
I escaped my grandmother's overfurnished house
for the hollow, cold smell of plaster, warm
smell of sawdust underfoot, shapes
of unfinished objects on clean shelves
as I entered at sunset.

All these dreams, this obsession with bare boards:
scaffolding, with only a few objects
in an ecstasy of space, where through the windows
the scent of pines can blow in, where we eat off the floor
laughing, like Japanese sages—How to begin?
O serenity
that can live without chairs, with only a mat,
maybe a crimson mat, or maybe not even...
old smell of clay on a wheel, new smell of boards
just cut, the ring of the sculptor's studio.

Where have I escaped from? What have I escaped to?
Why has my child no father?
I must be halfway up the circular stair.
To shape my own—
                    Friends! I hold out my hands
as all that light pours down, it is pouring down.

[1967-1983]

6
Dispossessions

1970-1973

Poetry As Continuity

The young doctor dreamed of revolution.
The middleaged revolutionary dreamed of a tree
offering its red berries, thrusting down roots like a woman.

Under miles of snow, under railroad tracks stitched like a
    suture,
the earth slept all the way to Moscow.
How strangely space is playing the part of time!

What reached the city was only a coincidence
in a life of parades. Zhivago,
you are all we have left, in the end you were scarcely a man.

Waiting

My body knows it will never bear children.
What can I say to my body now,
this used violin?
Every night it cries out strenuously
from its secret cave.

Old body, old friend,
why are you so unforgiving?

Why are you so stiff and resistant
clenched around empty space?
An instrument is not a box.

But suppose you are an empty box?
Suppose you are like that famous wooden music hall
    in Troy, New York,
waiting to be torn down
where the orchestras love to play?

Let compassion breathe in and out of you
filling you, singing

A Circle, a Square, a Triangle and a Ripple of Water

Sex floated like a moon
over the composition. Home
was transpierced, ego
thrust out of line and
shaded. But sex floated
over the unconscious, pulling it
up like a sea in points to
where she dreamed, rolling
on and on, immaculate, a full moon
or a breast full of milk.
Seemingly untouched she
was the stone at the center of
the pool whose circles
shuddered off around her.

Holding Out

Letters come, the phone rings, you sit by your window
balancing yourself like a last glass of water.

All over the city the hospitals are crammed with wounded.
Divorce, like marriage, requires two adversaries.

But what is left now is not to exaggerate:
your grief, his grief—these serious possessions.

Dispossessions

1 | THINGS

Things have their own lives here. The hall chairs
count me as I climb the steps. The piano
is playing at will from behind three potted plants,
while the photograph of the dead girl in the luminescent
 hat
glows pink since the lamp lighted itself at four.

We are very humane here. Of course people
go off course sometimes, radio to the outside world
only through typewriter noise or the bathwater running.
And then the empty glasses, the books on health food left
 around....
But the things have been here longer than we have.

And the trees are older even than furniture.
They were here to witness the original drownings
(because I always think the children drowned, no matter
 what you say).
Last night a voice called me from outside my door.
It was no one's voice, perhaps it came from the umbrella
 stand.

2 | SOUVENIRS

Anyway we are always waking
in bedrooms of the dead, smelling
musk of their winter jackets, tracking
prints of their heels across our blurred carpets.

So why hang onto a particular postcard?
If a child's lock of hair brings back
the look of that child, shall I
nevertheless not let it blow away?

Houses, houses, we lodge in such husks!
inhabit such promises, seeking the unborn
in a worn-out photograph, hoping to break free
even of our violent and faithful lives.

3 | INHERITANCES

Malte Laurids, peevish: *And one has*
nothing and nobody, travels about the world
with a few clothes and a satchel of books. What sort of life
is it? without a house, without
inheritances (the Chamberlain's eyeglasses, say,
in a glass case?), *without*
dogs—

Yet he wrote the Chamberlain's death, explaining:
I have taken action against fear, I
have sat all night and written.

And: *Still it is not enough*
to have memories, they
must turn to blood inside you.

Suicide Note

It's not that I'm out of touch—
a child stranded on a shoal
looking back without feeling
at the grownups still playing on the beach.

It's just that everyone else's
needs seem so urgent!
Already I've ceased to exist
at my end of this conversation—

And I wanted to defend you!
The telephone is the invader.
Wreath of electrodes! Love!
No trespassing beyond this point. Anyone found here
    with dog or gun will be

A Nightmare of the Suburbs

I'll be in my own room, upstairs,
the door locked, with a gun—
But nobody's coming
yet,

no black bodies
rising like night-flowers from your leafy summer streets,
no axe that splits
the drowsy thighbones of your window frame.

You look in your hand mirror—
They won't get in without a struggle!

But already the meager body
of the pistol begins to wake from his long sleep
of cardboard in the drawer of your bedside table.

Glowing blue-black,
now that he's here
only blood can appease him.

The Earthquake

Two people wakened suddenly by an earthquake
accuse each other: *You pushed me out of bed!*
The floor is cold, they're disgruntled, they start to laugh.
Back to bed. The little hills
just beginning to show dark along the horizon
fold their paws and shove off to sleep again
embracing privacy.

But what can I say for the one who sleeps alone
in a child's cot? *Another dream?*
She imagines she must have parachuted out of bed
to escape.
She accuses herself.
Stubbornly, in a mummy-roll of blankets,
she lies awake explaining her usual day.

Pencil Sketch of Self & Other

When you kissed me it was as if
someone had just stepped lightly out of the room.

How shy I was in any crowd,
and you, how adept!

How I kept you waiting
longer than any boy uncertain of his sex!

Your mother, musical, suicidal,
slept with a thread tied round her nurse's finger

(so I learned a few details), your rich father
photographed beside his swimming pool....

How we almost ruined each other, you
with your hope of children,

I with my body which I took too seriously,
that stunned room....

A story, like *The Garden Party*,
no longer even possible.

Yet I want to forgive us both
as if it still matters.

7
The Flashboat

1975-1983

The Flashboat

1

A high deck. Blue skies overhead. White distance.
The wind on my tongue. A day of days. From the shore a
    churchbell clangs.
Below me the grinding of floes: tiny families huddled
    together
earth-colored. Let me explain, the ice is cracking free.
They were cut off unawares. From the shore a churchbell
    clangs.
When the ice breaks up it is spring. No
comfort, no comfort.

2

And here is that part of my dream I would like to forget. The
purser is at his desk, he is leaning toward me out of his seat,
he is my torturer who assumes we think alike. Again and
again he questions me as to which national boundaries I
plan to cross. *Are you a political activist? No, I'm a teacher.*
But already the last villagers have been swept out to sea.
We are cruising north of the Arctic Circle. Without haste he
locks my passport away in his breast pocket. Was I wrong
to declare myself innocent?

3

(I did not protest. I spoke nothing but the truth. I never
spoke of that girl who kneeled by her skyscraper window,
falling without a sound through the New York City night.)

4

Now it's our turn. Three a.m.
and the Queen Mary is sinking.
All is bustle—but in grays. Red lanterns crawl here and
    there.
The crew makes ready the boats. One near me, broad but
    shallow,
looks safe, women are urged, the captain will be in charge.
Far down now: a trough. A smaller dory rocks
in and out of our lights; black fists grip the oars.
Room only for six—we will
all need to row.
For a moment I hesitate, worrying about my defective blood.
A rope ladder drops over. My voice with its crunch of bone
wakes me: *I choose*
the flashboat!
           work,
                 the starry waters

A Mission with the Night

*An old black man used to come to our door in
Florida during the Depression. He never got lost
going home through the dark without a flashlight.
He would say, "I got a mission wid' de night."*

1

She is like that man
She is like that man carrying his torch of words
She is like the torch of words
She is the poet with her torch of words in exile
She is in exile
She is finding her way
She is finding her way home through a cypress swamp
She is finding her way back on a moonless night
She is like the moon
She is like a ray of the moon or a cypress root
She is like the root uncovering its own source
She is like the ray at an open window
She is an open window
She is not at the source yet
The source is finding her out

2

He came all this way
leaning on his old stick like a flame
a jointed flame, a flame that hums with words

The words soaked up from the earth itself
They reached his fingers, they signified to his heart
They became his eyes that reached into the night

He is at the door
He is standing at the old screen door with his one yellow
     tooth
smiling, asking for food

Jittoku, Buddhist Mystic—15th Century

Everything is blowing, his
skirts are blowing, he stands
hands clasped in enormous sleeves
behind his back, at his feet a
dropped broom. The strokes of the
broom made of dry sticks and the
swoop of a few live pine needles
shiver together, his unruly
chopped-off hair and the fringes
of his girdle all are blowing
eastward. Only the corners of his
mouth defy gravity. He is laughing,
humped against the wind with his bawdy
nostrils wide he is laughing: The
moon! Old boat of the white full moon!

Rent

If you want my apartment, sleep in it
but let's have a clear understanding:
the books are still free agents.

If the rocking chair's arms surround you
they can also let you go,
they can shape the air like a body.

I don't want your rent, I want
a radiance of attention
like the candle's flame when we eat,

I mean a kind of awe
attending the spaces between us—
Not a roof but a field of stars.

Conversation by the Body's Light

Out of my poverty
Out of your poverty
Out of your nakedness
Out of my nakedness
Between the swimmer in the water
And the watcher of the skies
Something is altered

Something is offered
Something is breathed
The body's radiance
Like the points of a constellation
Beckons to insight
Here is my poverty:
A body hoarded
Ridiculous in middle age
Unvoiced, unpracticed

And here is your poverty:
A prodigality
That guts its source
The self picked clean
In its shining houses

Out of my nakedness
Out of your nakedness
Between the swimmer in the skies
And the watcher from the water
Something is reached
For a moment, acknowledged
Lost—or is it shelter?
The still not-believed-in
Heartbeat of the glacier

Praise

But I love this poor earth,
because I have not seen another....

—OSIP MANDELSTAM

Between five and fifty
most people construct a little lifetime:
they fall in love, make kids, they suffer
and pitch the usual tents of understanding.
But I have built a few unexpected bridges.
Out of inert stone, with its longing to embrace inert stone,
I have sent a few vaults into stainless air.
Is this enough—when I love our poor sister earth?
Sister earth, I kneel and ask pardon.
A clod of turf is no less than inert stone.
Nothing is enough!
In this field set free for our play
who could have foretold
I would live to write at fifty?

Flute Song

Earth-spirit, wood-spirit, stone,
father, Other, exposed root
I said goodbye to by the river, where
are you now? I fondle a glass eye.

The eye reflects leaves, stars,
galaxies.... Space
was always my demon, the unreachable.
From a black hole, a wavering
flute song, readable.

The Blue Anchor

The future weighs down on me
just like a wall of light!

All these years
I've lived by necessity.
Now the world shines
like an empty room
clean all the way to the rafters.

The room might be waiting for its first tenants—
a bed, a chair, my old typewriter.

Or it might be Van Gogh's room
at Arles:
so neat, while his eyes grazed among phosphorus.
A blue anchor.

To live in the future
like a survivor!
Not the first step up the beach
but the second
then the third

—never forgetting
the wingprint of the mountain
over the fragile human settlement—

Threads: Rosa Luxemburg from Prison

1 | WRONKE, SPRING 1917

You ask what I am reading. Natural science
for the most part; I am studying the distribution
of plants and animals.

A huge white poplar half fills the prison garden.
All the songbirds love that tree best. The young leaves
sticky all over with a white down
shine in the sun like flowers!
But by now the small birds
(May 23rd) are much too busy to sing.
Hens keep their nests, cocks with their beaks full
streak back and forth. Yesterday—
yes, for the first time in almost three weeks
I caught the *zeezeebey!* of a blue tit
shrilling over the wall.
At fourteen I was proud, I pitied my mother
for telling me Solomon understood the gossip of birds.
Now I'm like Solomon, that quick *zeezeebey!*
roused me to the sorrows of bird life

I must be out of sorts, just now I was reading
how in the name of scientific agriculture
we've drained the swamps, chopped down brushwood
    and stumps,
cleared away leaves,
while civilized men (according to Professor Sieber)
drove the Redskins from their feeding grounds
in North America

And they made you talk to Karl
through a grating?
I remember in Warsaw
I was on hunger strike, I could barely stand.

112

My brother came to see me. They propped me in a cage,
a cage within a cage. (I gripped with both hands
to hold myself upright.) From the outer wires
he peered across as at a zoo. *Where are you?* he asked,
again and again brushing away the tears that clouded his
     glasses

But you make too much of my "equanimity," Sonya.
It is simply my way
when I suffer not to utter a word

Sonyusha, I know I can say this to you, my darling—
You will not promptly accuse me
of treason against socialism. Suppose I am really
not a human being at all but some bird or beast?
I walk up and down my scrap of prison garden—
I'm alone in a field where the grass is humming with
     bees—
and I feel more at home
than at a party congress. Of course I always
mean to die at my post, in a street fight
or prison. But my first self
belongs to the tomtits more than to our comrades

Still, nature is cruel, not a refuge,
and—you won't mind?—I have to laugh
a little when you ask me, *How can men dare
judge you and Karl?* My little bird,
given the totality of vital forms
through twenty thousand years of civilization,
that's not a reasonable question! Why are there blue tits?
Zeezeebey! but I'm awfully glad there are.
We live in the painfulest moment of evolution,
the very chapter of change, and you have to ask,
What is the meaning of it all? Listen,
one day I found a beetle stunned on its back,
its legs gnawed to stumps by ants; another day
I clambered to free a peacock butterfly
battering half dead inside our bathroom pane.

113

Locked up myself after six, I lean on the sill.
The sky's like iron, a heavy rain falls, the nightingale
sings in the sycamore as if possessed.
What is the meaning of it all? What is the meaning
of young weeds tufted in the prison wall? young poplar
   shoots?
underground passages of wasp and wild bee
I try not to shake when I walk? ant highways
straight as the Roman? The wall stones shine with wet,
reddish, bluish—a comfort even on
color-starved winter days—gray and resurgent green

2 | BRESLAU, NOVEMBER-DECEMBER 1917

I had a vision of all the splendor of war!

Hans is killed
        Now twilight begins at four
N "broke the news"
           Over the great paved courtyard
           hundreds of rooks fly by with a rowing stroke
Such a parade of grief! Why can't friends understand
I need solitude to consider? Why not tell me
quickly, briefly, simply
so as not to cheapen
           Their homecoming caw,
           throaty and muted, is so different from their
           sharp morning caw after food. As if metal balls,
           tossed from one to the other, high in the air,
           tinkled   exchanging the day's news
my last two letters
addressed to a dead man
           stolen greetings
           passed between me and the rooks
           here in the darkening yard
I'm allowed so few letters. But from now on, Sonitchka,
I can talk to you again—I mean on paper—
just as before

If only I could send you
like a starry cloak
the confident joy I feel. I lie awake
in black wrappings of boredom, unfreedom and cold.
A distant train hoots. Now there's the squeak
of damp gravel under the desolate boot

of the midnight guard, who coughs. It becomes a song.
My cell trembles. I'm lying in a field streaked with light.
How can that be? My heart beats. Life itself,
the riddle, becomes the key to the riddle. Even this war,
this huge asylum, this casual misery
in which we drown, this too must be transformed
into something meant, heroic. Like an elemental force,
some flood or hurricane, like an eclipse of the sun,
absurd to judge it! These are the chosen tracks
down which the future must break forth. If only the war
    lasts....
Meanwhile, I'm deep in geology.
You may find that dry, but it opens up
the vastest conception of nature, the most unified view
of any science. I read
in an intoxication of calm. I look up
to smile at Hans as if he stood in the door.
These forces, these cataclysms that would sweep us away,
we have to accept them
as subjects of study, data for exploration

Eagles, falcons, hawks, owls   All the birds of prey
flying to Egypt   Bird migrations
always a puzzle to me
over the blue Mediterranean
        From Rumania: war trophies
        A hundred head of buffalo
        in Breslau alone
        These beasts, stronger than oxen
        Their horns recurved
        over a skull flat as a sheep's
        Black hide   Huge, soft eyes
Flying with them   so many that the sky floods dark:
nightingales, larks, golden-crested wrens
A cloud of songbirds
Thousands of natural victims
without fear
        Rough army drays

drawn up in the courtyard where I take my walks
The load: haversacks, old army tunics, shirts
darkened, soaked with blood
Brought here from the front
for the women prisoners to mend
All of them flying toward a common goal:
to drop half dead
beside the Nile
and sort themselves into territories and species
           Today a towering dray
           dragged by a team of freshly broken beasts
           The soldier-driver
           beating and beating with the butt of his whip
           Even our woman gatekeeper protesting
           One ripped and bleeding
           its stiff hide torn
           the look on its black face like a weeping child's
           The rest of the team
           half dead   standing while the dray was
              emptied at last
           perfectly still
Reading
how on the long flight south larger birds
often carry the small   Reading:
cranes
sighted in amazing numbers along the coast
with a twittering freight
of songbirds on their backs
           Eyes
           of the bleeding   My own dark
           handsomely photographed eyes
           Tears / negative
           Tears / negative
           Tears / negative   of my own face dead
           skull beaten in and
           drowned
The suffering of a dearly loved brother could hardly have
affected me more profoundly

As if all the birds declared
>Brother! I am one with your
a "truce of God!"
>>one with your pain, your helplessness, your
>>>longing
>>one with you in my helplessness

>>>The music of the songbirds
>>>in the flowery meadows of Rumania
>>>The mythical herdsman's call

*Meanwhile the women prisoners were jostling one another
as they busily unloaded the dray and carried the heavy
sacks into the administration building. The driver, hands
in his pockets, was striding up and down the courtyard
smiling to himself as he whistled a popular air. I had a
vision of all the splendor of war!*

3 | BRESLAU, SPRING 1918

*I am so looking forward to spring. It is the only
thing one never gets tired of.*

My window looks on the red brick wall
of the men's prison
           My petition for release
           has been rejected
Just the crests of trees
blur above the roofs of the lunatic asylum
           My petition   even for a brief furlough
           rejected
Here, unfortunately, that is all one can see
over the high brick wall
           It seems I am going to stay here
           till we have conquered the whole world

This lovely world! If only we could walk through it, talk
freely together, weep over it. Sonyusha,
whenever I don't hear from you, I fear you're driven,
whipped by the winds of your loneliness,
helpless as a young leaf. The days grow long,
the clouds rush by. Our chalky soil,
which doesn't yet show it's been planted,
streams with changing lights. Get out as much as you can.
Darling, the earth is faithful, the one thing
fresh but yet faithful. Be my eyes for me,
let me see all you see

This March seems fateful. Strange, to hear them singing
far off from the grounds of the lunatic asylum:
nightingales, wrynecks, golden orioles
(that "Whitsun bird"), never heard till April here,

119

never heard till May   laughing and
fluting in the
pale gray light
before dawn
What is the reason for this premature migration?
Is it meant for Berlin too?
Sonya, for my sake
please go to the Botanical Gardens,
let me hear all you hear,
for over and above the outcome of the Battle of Cambrai,
this really seems to me
the most important issue of the day

May 12th. Fragments of the established world
flame and submerge, they tear away. Day by day
we witness fresh catastrophes   Strange
how most people see nothing, most people
feel the earth firm under their feet when it is
flaming
*whereas my concern for organic nature is by now almost
morbid in its intensity*
Dusk: down below in the court
a young crested lark is running with short steps,
fluttering up and piping. I listen for the soft *hweet! hweet!*
of the parent birds seeking food. It makes me ill
to see such suffering
        I feel how you   must be suffering
and I can do nothing to help
My buffaloes still come, my foolish starling
is missing
        suffering because you can't "live"
sparrows and pigeons
follow me about like dogs
for a crumb
*It's no use telling myself I am not responsible for all the
hungry little larks in the world. Logic does not help*
        Never mind, we shall live   shall live
        through grand events
        Have patience

120

Thus passing out of my cell in all directions
are fine threads connecting me
with thousands of birds and beasts
         You too, Sonitchka, are one of this urgent
            company
         to which my whole self throbs, responsive
Write soon. Please tell me how Karl is.
Perhaps Pfemfert can find you *The Flax Field*
by Streuvels. For these Flemish authors
not Flanders alone has become the beloved
but all nature   beyond even
the radiant skin
of the globe

NOTES

FOREWORD: Stanzas have been dropped from "Letters" and "No More Elegies." The poems not previously published in book form include, besides the five "reclaimed" poems, "Song" and "Holding Out."

1

MERCATOR'S WORLD: Mercator (1512-1594) originated the projection that is still widely used for navigators' maps of the world. "*Mercator's projection* is of great value to navigators, since it shows true directions, but it has great disadvantages for general use. The parallels and meridians are represented as straight lines, intersecting at right angles.... In a MAP on Mercator's projection, Greenland appears larger than South America.... Of course, also, it is impossible to represent at all the areas very near the poles." (*The Columbia Encyclopedia*, 1945.)

AFTER THE BOMB TESTS, *page 10*: Specifically, the United States tests at Bikini Atoll in the Marshall Islands, Western Pacific, 1946. Kepler (1571-1630) formulated the laws of planetary motion.

2

NOTHING HAS BEEN USED IN THE MANUFACTURE OF THIS POETRY....: This essay was written to introduce the "Mercator's World" poems when they first appeared in *Maps & Windows*. Adrienne Rich's "When We Dead Awaken: Writing As Re-vision" (1971), now available in her book *On Lies, Secrets, and Silence*, was in many ways central to my thinking.

page 19: See Tillie Olsen's 1962 talk/essay, now reprinted as "Silences in Literature" at the beginning of her book *Silences*. Olsen lists the important women writers of the nineteenth century who never married and points to the surprisingly large number even in this century who have remained single or, at any rate, childless.
page 19: John Berryman: *The Dream Songs*, number 187.
page 26: "Now that we turn against the whole notion...." How I wish "we" did! But I have not wanted to change the original course of this argument.

page 31: Elizabeth Bishop has since become one of my necessary poets—as has Berrryman.

page 39: Anaïs Nin: *Diary of Anaïs Nin, 1934-39*. The whole passage reads: "Rank believes that to create it is necessary to destroy. Woman cannot destroy. He believes that may be why she has rarely been a great artist. In order to create without destroying, I nearly destroyed myself."

4

FEATHERS, page 71: The first line, like the over-all title "March," comes from Zhivago's sequence of poems at the end of Pasternak's *Doctor Zhivago* (poems translated by Bernard Guilbert Guerney).

HUNGER MOON, page 72: In February, 1967, *The New York Times* noted that in the Middle West the last full moon before the spring equinox used to be called the "hunger moon," because it was still too early to plant, yet there was not enough feed left in the barns for the animals. However, I suspect this expression goes back to the Native Americans.

EL SUEÑO DE LA RAZÓN, page 73: A nightmare etching by Goya is inscribed "El sueño de la razón produce monstruos"—"The dream of reason begets monsters."

MIDDLE AGE, page 77: The line "Only the miracle is real" comes from Lukács but suggests much in Pasternak, for instance, "In real life, I thought, everything must be a miracle" (from *I Remember*, chapter on "Scriabin").

6

INHERITANCES, page 95: Quoted virtually in its entirety from Rilke's *The Notebooks of Malte Laurids Brigge*, translated by M.D. Herter Norton.

7

JITTOKU, BUDDHIST MYSTIC..., page 106: See, in the Boston Museum of Fine Arts, "Jittoku, a Buddhist Mystic, Laughing at the Moon" (School of Geiami, 1432-1485).

PRAISE, *page 109*: The image of stone as the poet's building material, and the phrase about the world's being set free for our play during the two thousand years of Christian civilization, are both taken from Osip Mandelstam, as reported by Nadezhda Mandelstam in *Hope Against Hope*, chapter 56, "The Earth and Its Concerns." The chapter begins: "A woman who has come back after many years in the forced-labor camps tells me that she and her companions in misfortune always found comfort in the poetry which, luckily, she knew by heart and was able to recite to them. They were particularly moved by some lines M. wrote as a young man: *But I love this poor earth, because I have not seen another....*"

THREADS, *page 112*: This poem is based on Rosa Luxemburg's *Prison Letters to Sophie Liebknecht*, the wife of her friend and co-revolutionary Karl Liebknecht. Together Rosa Luxemburg and Karl Liebknecht founded the Spartacus League and opposed the Kaiser's war policy, and they spent almost the whole of World War I as political prisoners in various German prisons. Both were released a few days before the Armistice, only to be picked up again by government authorities, interrogated, and killed. Rosa Luxemburg was beaten about the head, shot, and her body dumped in a canal. Her friend Hans Dieffenbach, a doctor, was killed at the front.

ACKNOWLEDGMENTS

Grateful acknowledgment is made to the Macmillan Publishing Company of New York and Collier Macmillan Canada, Ltd., for permission to reprint much of *The Weather of Six Mornings* in Parts 3 and 4 of this book and of *Maps & Windows* in Parts 1, 2, and 6.

In addition, my thanks to the editors of the following magazines and anthologies, where many of the poems first appeared: *The American Poetry Review*, *The Antioch Review*, *Green House*, *The Nation*, *New World Writing*, *Pequod*, *Ploughshares*, *Poetry* (Chicago), *Poetry London-New York*, *Sarah Lawrence Alumnae Magazine*, *Sarah Lawrence Journal*, *The Transatlantic Review*, *Voices*, *Voyages*, *Westigan Review of Poetry*; also *American Poems*, ed. Jascha Kessler (Southern Illinois University Press), *New Poets of England and America, Second Selection*, eds. Donald Hall and Robert Pack (Meridian Books), and *No More Masks*, eds. Florence Howe and Ellen Bass (Doubleday Anchor Books). "Morning on the St. John's," "The Weather of Six Mornings," "Feathers" under the title "March," and "No More Elegies," all in slightly different versions, and "The Flashboat" appeared originally in *The New Yorker*.

The prose of Part 2 appeared originally in *The American Poetry Review*.

"Threads" was first published by Flamingo Press, New York, for the benefit of the White House Lawn Eleven, an anti-nuclear group of the War Resisters League. For permission to quote from the text of Rosa Luxemburg's *Prison Letters to Sophie Liebknecht*, translated from the German by Eden and Cedar Paul, on which the poem is based, I am indebted to Independent Labour Publications, Leeds.

I am grateful to the John Simon Guggenheim Memorial Foundation, the Ingram Merrill Foundation, the Creative Artists Public Service Program of New York State, and the National Endowment for the Arts for grants and fellowships that gave me time and freedom in which to write, and to the MacDowell Colony in Peterborough, New Hampshire, and Yaddo in Saratoga Springs, New York, where much work was actually done.